WHAT MAKES
BOYS TOWN
Successful

A Description of the 21st Century
Boys Town Teaching Model

WHAT MAKES BOYS TOWN
Successful

A Description of the 21st Century
Boys Town Teaching Model

Val J. Peter

BOYS
TOWN
PRESS

What Makes Boys Town Successful

Published by the Boys Town Press
Father Flanagan's Boys' Home
Boys Town, Nebraska 68010

Publisher's Cataloging-in-Publication
(Prepared by Quality Books, Inc.)

Peter, Val J.
    What makes Boys Town successful : a description of the 21st century Boys Town teaching model / Val J. Peter.
      p. cm.
    ISBN: 1-889322-26-1

    1. Father Flanagan's Boys' Home. 2. Behavior therapy for children. 3. Teaching. I. Father Flanagan's Boys' Home. II. Title.

HV876.P48 1999   362.7'4'09782254
                                     QBI98-1593

9810-19-0001

10   9   8   7   6   5   4   3   2   1

Table of Contents

Introduction

*A*s we enter the 21st century, there is an enormous storm blowing across the American landscape with gale force winds. There isn't a family or school that hasn't suffered from its prolonged effects.

Usually when terrible storms come our way, people (and child-care institutions, too) retreat to their inner sanctuaries, lock the doors, close the shutters, and take care of themselves as they ride out the storm.

Not so at Boys Town. Instead of retreating, we have plunged ourselves in the midst of the storm moving forward, looking for America's throw-away children. We are expanding both the locations and types of our programs to help more children and families at a time when many other homes for children are closing because of the storm. Yes, we're out there in the storm moving forward for the sake of the children at grave risk. We have set fear and timidity aside. We are taking great risks ourselves.

Are we making mistakes as we go? Yes, lots of them. Even though we know we are moving in the right direction, the storm is so bad that we often cannot see in front of our face. Every risk-taker does this. But our faith helps us. Our experience gives us confidence we're moving in the right direction, and our courage helps us get up when we fall and begin anew.

We know of no other child-care agency in America that is taking these kinds of risks for these children in the midst of the storm. Oh, yes, there are plenty of rescue missions, and they do good work. But we don't just rescue. Our main business is beyond rescue. It's rehabilitation. Our mission is to teach kids skills, help them build relationships, and empower at-risk youth in such a way that they can take control of their own lives and not let anger, frustration, drugs, violence, or even mental illness dictate their actions and their future. We want to help kids put an end to the cycle of hurting others and hurting themselves as well. It's not easy to teach kids how to do this in the midst of gale force winds. That's where many of them are today.

For many years judges, probation officers, social workers, legislators, and most especially parents and friends of at-risk boys and girls have asked us questions such as these: Why do you have such success with children whom so many have given up on? How do you do it? What is your secret? Will you share it with us?

Although we are far from perfect and not successful with every youngster in our care, we really do have something special here at Boys Town. The basic research which grounds our approach was done at Kansas University almost thirty years ago. We at Boys Town took their work, expanded it, enlarged it, and developed it far beyond. But we don't want to keep it a secret.

This present little book is not a technical manual or blueprint showing the reader the necessary details of putting the Boys Town Model in place. You acquire that knowledge and skill only by going through our training and consultation programs. Its more modest purpose is just as important, namely, to help you understand and conceptualize our ways of providing quality care and treatment for America's needy children and families.

We hope many of you will spread the word: many abandoned, abused, and deeply troubled children, adolescents, and families can be helped to rebuild their lives and their faith in themselves. They can take charge of themselves once again. We hope some of you who run programs for children and families will seek the technical assistance Boys Town is willing and eager to share with you. We hope all of you will go away from this experience feeling hopeful for the abandoned, abused, neglected, and troubled children of America and their families. There is no such thing as a bad boy or girl. There is always room for hope.

Chapter 1

Developmental History of the Boys Town Model

*T*o understand the concept of helping children learn new behaviors, one must first realize that we are in the "business" of bringing healing and hope to children and families. Everything we do is rooted in the human experience – the successes, the failures, the progress, the obstacles. Children are human beings, not products on an assembly line. And we at Boys Town are caregivers, not robots programmed to perform the same task, the same way, every day. It is true that technology and theory are necessary, but so are genuine compassion, concern, and lots of common sense. In helping at-risk children, technology without love is pure manipulation. And love without good science is pure sentimentality. I wish lots of love would make them better, all by itself. But it usually doesn't work that way with today's youth.

Ours is a noble cause – to help children gain the knowledge, the skills, and the ability to make wise decisions that will enable them to find success in their lives. We are teaching them to take charge of their own lives. Achieving those lofty goals requires dedicated people armed with extraordinary tools. That's where the history of the Boys Town Teaching Model begins.

While the Boys Town Teaching Model has its basis in learning theory, it has not adopted a "mechanistic" view of how a child learns as have several other models that take this approach. In the Boys Town Model, the child is an active participant in the teaching and learning that occurs. The goal is self-control and empowerment. The child isn't merely told how to behave; he or she learns positive behaviors and how to choose to use them in many different situations. This "empowerment," or self-help approach, combines the active participation of the child with the active teaching of the parent or caretaker. The strength of this approach is that it teaches children prosocial skills and helps them build healthy relationships with others while putting them back in charge of their own lives.

So the overall goal of the Boys Town Model is to teach a child how to learn self-help skills and build positive relationships, both of which result in intrinsic changes within the child. We don't want to be in charge or in control except as a start – in order for children to take control of their own lives. By learning self-help, children can change the way they think, feel, and act.

This is a learning process. Boys Town's teaching methods utilize behavioral principles, while allowing children to integrate their thoughts and feelings into this learning process. Unlike many other learning theory models, Boys Town uses external reinforcement, where appropriate, to promote and maintain skill learning and relationship development. This allows children to change intrinsically. Inadequate thought patterns change, negative feelings diminish, and inappropriate behaviors change to positive ones for the youth and others.

Over the years, the Boys Town Model has been changing and moving ahead. It does not remain static or fixed. This means that we regularly incorporate what we are learning from our clinical work with children and families, or from research that reveals new information about the problems children face and how to address them. But while our model is open to change, some things remain permanent: our solid behavioral base, our emphasis on internalization and generalization, our spiritual and moral foundations, and our reliance on research and clinical learning. Let's look back on the "life" of our Model and compare its development to that of a child.

When raising very small children, moms and dads rightly place tight restrictions on their environments at times and set limits as to where they can and cannot go ("Don't play with fire." "Don't go out of the yard." "Don't cross the street."). Similarly, physicians place sharp restrictions on patients ("Don't walk on that foot." "Stay in bed for five days.") so that healing may take place. We at Boys Town do the same thing when a child first comes to us. It may appear that we are rigid. We are governed by rules that create a carefully structured environment. We set these tight boundaries to help the healing process so the child can learn self-control. Our children's ability to reason isn't very good when they come to us. So it is our responsibility to help them.

When the Boys Town Model was "born" in 1975, we took this basic approach. The Model had its origins in a research project called Achievement Place, conducted at Kansas University in the late 1960s and early 1970s. Boys Town adopted this work, expanded it, and developed it far beyond.

Like good parents, we were protective of our new approach and its boundaries and set very clear expectations and limits. Some may have regarded these as too strict, not realizing that in the early stages of development they were necessary to ensure continuation and progress of the Model. Since it was so new, it was important to strictly adhere to its components and apply it "by the book." Those early days were a time of cautious, steady growth for the Model. And just as parents must act to protect their children, Boys Town acted to safeguard the clear successes we were having with children.

At the same time, Boys Town remained open to change. As the Model grew – just as a child grows – we developed, incorporated, and generated new ideas, learned from research and experience, and began to find new ways to help children. This explains how the Model can have permanent elements, which ensures that the caregivers continue to use it as it was meant to be used, and still experience change, which encourages program development and improvement to help children and families.

It is important here to remember how our mission of caring for children started. Boys Town began taking in needy and troubled children in 1917, when Father Edward Flanagan founded his home for boys in Omaha, Nebraska. In those early days, Father Flanagan established three basic principles for the type of care he would provide for "his boys." These three are what we would call his "program," his "child-care technology": education, vocational training, and self-government.

First, Father Flanagan believed that youngsters should not be sent to the jails of his time but could be rehabilitated through education. This started with the three R's – reading, 'riting, and 'rithmetic, with a strong emphasis on religious education as well. Second, every boy needed a vocation or trade, something that would enable him to make a living. Father Flanagan knew that if kids wanted to be productive members of society, each and every one of them needed to be trained with some marketable skill: a shoemaker, barber, printer, electrician, carpenter, butcher, baker, etc.

Third, Father Flanagan believed that his boys needed to practice self-government. The youth elected their own mayor, councilmen, and other officers, and everyone had an active voice in the Home's operation. In today's parlance, we could call this "empowerment." Father Flanagan passionately believed in freedom, equality, and justice, and welcomed boys of all races, creeds, and colors to live and learn in the Boys Town family.

Together, these three areas made up the child-care technology of Boys Town in the early days. Father Flanagan's Home had not only a "head" (these three elements) but also a big "heart." Yes, the other half of the genius of Boys Town was a big heart, namely, the love for children that was his enduring legacy.

From 1917 on, this approach benefited thousands of young people who were able to change their lives for the better at Boys Town. But the world changed drastically in the 1960s: cities burned down, the Vietnam war almost destroyed our nation, and drugs became a way of life for many as families began to fall apart. In the late 1960s and early 1970s youngsters started coming to Boys Town with new problems – physical, emotional, and sexual abuse, drugs, alcohol, suicide, and violence of all sorts. And these problems could not be "fixed" by the three R's, vocational training, and self-government. And love alone could not bring hope and healing. Our "head" was gone. We only had a "heart." It wasn't enough. We looked across America for something that was working. There wasn't anything. Oh, positive peer culture was starting to develop, but it had no family structure. So we were on our own.

What we needed was a new approach, a new set of child-care technologies for a new generation of children in need. Keep in mind that the heart without the head is pure sentimentality. And the head without the heart is pure manipulation. It was out of this need that the Boys Town Model was created.

The Model grew and prospered in the 1970s and early 1980s. So successful did it become that two kinds of expansion were called for: first, geographic expansion, and second, technology transfer to new programs.

So in 1985, monumental changes occurred as Boys Town began a national expansion to major metropolitan areas across the country. There was one big question to be answered regarding geographic expansion: how would the Model work in New York City, Los Angeles, and other geographic settings? Could the Model really be replicated there? We began to see this question answered with positive results as we established Boys Town programs far away from "the little house on the prairie."

Then in 1988 we began technology transfer. We expanded the Model to include four new service areas: parent training, in-home services, emergency shelter services, and treatment foster care. In 1990, training programs were added, including educational training and hospital services. We discovered that the technology could be transferred from one program to another, and it was effective.

The combination of our nationwide expansion and the creation of new programs flooded the Model with a wealth of new information, new ideas, and new technology. This resulted in more change and set the stage for another cycle of evolution within the Model, beginning in 1996.

Learning how to do things better requires change. But our desire to change has not meant abandoning the basic principles and ideas that have made our Model so effective and so attractive. As we have developed new ways of teaching kids, training caregivers, and promoting programs, we simply built (and continue to build) on the behavioral base of what we know works best for children and families.

Earlier, we compared the growth of the Boys Town Model to that of a developing child. Using that analogy again, a child is constantly growing – physically, emotionally, and intellectually. This child's world is different from what it was when he was a toddler. There are new things to experience and new ways to interact with the people in his life. Yet, almost everything this child does is firmly rooted in the lessons he learned and the experiences he had earlier in life. He retains and remembers the basic rules and boundaries, and builds upon them as he develops and grows.

When Father Flanagan founded his Home for orphaned and wayward boys in 1917, he knew they would respond to kindness, compassion, and discipline. They did. More than 80 years later, even amid the mind-boggling array of problems our youth face, these are still the qualities that help young boys and girls turn their lives around.

As we said earlier, the major constants of the Boys Town Model are teaching skills, building relationships, and empowerment. Teaching skills is what helps kids learn new ways of thinking, new ways of feeling good, and new ways of behaving. By teaching, we give kids the skills they need in order to take control of their lives and be successful. Whether it's a parent who wants to teach her daughter the skill of problem-solving, or a staff member in a youth shelter trying to help a youth learn anger-control strategies, teaching is the key.

At the same time, helping children build relationships enables them to feel better about themselves and their lives and to feel more hopeful for the future. In addition, a strong relationship creates a bond of trust between a caregiver and a youth. A child is much more likely to learn from and try to imitate an adult who is warm, fun to be with, sincere, and caring. Many of the kids who come to Boys Town have been in hurtful relationships. They have learned to be mistrustful. They have a hard time getting along with others as well. Reaching out to a child and helping the child remove the layers of distrust and anger that have built up over time is one of the most difficult, and at the same time, promising tasks there is. But once a child responds, and realizes that someone has his or her best interests at heart, progress is swift and the rewards are great for both the youth and the caregiver. If a child feels he has a say in his own education and treatment, he has a head start on the road to healing and hope.

The spirit of both continuity and change have brought Boys Town to where it is today. We realize that just as there will always be children and families who need help, there will always be better ways to help them. And while the Boys Town Teaching Model was built on the lessons of the past, it needs to always keep its sights set firmly on the future as well.

"The work will continue, you see, whether I am there or not, because it is God's work, not mine."
—Father Edward Flanagan

Chapter 2

The Boys Town Family Home Program

*W*hen most people think of Boys Town, they still look to the village in Nebraska, founded on December 10, 1917, by Father Edward J. Flanagan, as inspiring and energetic a figure as ever walked the shores of America.

Father Flanagan had himself experienced oppression, rejection, sickness, and a sense of failure as a youngster. His family emigrated from Ireland to get away from the repressive control of their island by a foreign power. Upon arriving on the shores of America, he sought to become a priest in the prestigious Archdiocese of New York. He was rejected as a "rather sickly lad of little promise." That's what the monsignor who interviewed him for the Archdiocese of New York wrote down. So he came to the Middle West. "Go out to Nebraska. They take anybody out there."

The Bishop of Omaha quickly recognized his potential and sent him off to Rome to study. There sickness befell him, and he came home as a failure, wondering whether he would ever regain health enough to pursue the goal of priesthood. He worked in the packing plants. He knew what discouragement meant. He tried again and this time was sent to study in Innsbruck, Austria, where he flourished.

When he returned to Nebraska as a newly ordained priest, he started working with homeless men who were on the streets. Here again he experienced failure. And that's when, in the midst of all of this discouragement and lack of success, he founded a home where orphaned and neglected boys could be helped. He wanted it to be a real home, and he set out with great faith in God to build what he called "the City of Little Men." As Boys Town came to serve more and more children, Father Flanagan's dormitories were, in his own opinion, only a start. "I still don't have it right," he said. "It needs to be more like a family."

With the grace of God, Boys Town pioneered a new model of family home care in the 1970s. We called it the Boys Town Family Home Program.

The core of our Family Home Program is our children. Every child who comes to Boys Town brings with him or her a broken heart and shattered dreams.

The dreams have been shattered by untold troubles and tragedies: perhaps mental illness, physical abuse, psychological abuse, sexual abuse, divorce, abandonment, alcoholism, poverty, poor companions, delinquency, promiscuity, drugs, broken homes, poor schools, or poor example. But there are other dreams. The dream of a second chance, the dream of a place so supportive, so loving, and so helpful that a troubled kid whom everyone has given up on has a real honest-to-goodness opportunity to be healed and to grow into a better person, a happy, successful, contributing member of society.

This is the goal of Boys Town as established by its founder, Father Flanagan, in 1917 and carried on to this day by all who live and work at Boys Town. It is a dream founded on great faith, hope, and love. It is being fulfilled each day in the lives of every boy and girl at the Home. It is the most cherished commodity in every Boys Town program. Why? Because it is what makes the Boys Town Model work.

Family-Teachers

Each home at the various Boys Town sites across America is staffed by two full-time Family-Teachers (a specially trained married couple who live in the home with up to eight youths) and a full-time Assistant Family-Teacher. They have the incredible task of working with children who have long histories of failure and attempting to prepare them for a more successful future. They not only work with each child in the home environment but they also work with the parents, teachers, social agencies, and churches involved with their youths. The Family-Teachers are the key to quality care. Many apply, but few meet the test. They are "the bold, the proud, the few."

We all have asked young children what they want to be when they grow up. We have all heard about kids who want to be firemen, doctors, nurses, policemen, lawyers, teachers, ministers, priests, husbands, and wives – but not many have said, "I want to be a Family-Teacher" or a "child-care worker." Why? Some experts indicate that the profession of child-care workers is still in its infancy or just beginning to emerge therefrom. Standardized, formal training programs are not widely used. In addition, licensure, certification, and career ladders are not typical. As a result, child-care workers frequently have very little authority and do not enjoy the same respect as do other human service professionals.

Family-Teachers at Boys Town are different from shift staff. Their Boys Town home is their home. They don't just work there and "then go to some other place that is called 'home.'" They are different from houseparents because Family-Teachers are the primary treatment agents for the children in their family.

At Boys Town, Family-Teachers are well-respected professionals because of the importance of their role and the quality of care they provide. To assure the development of their professional skills they participate in a rigorous, ongoing training program. This begins with preservice training to prepare Family-Teachers to enter a home. The training process then continues by means of consultation by clinical specialists who assist Family-Teachers to improve their skills. Each year Family-Teachers must meet Boys Town's high standards in order to be certified or recertified as professional Family-Teachers. If they do not meet these rigorous standards, they are "helped out" of the program. Family-Teachers have considerable authority, autonomy, and accountability. Boys Town wants to make sure they have the skills they need to work successfully with kids!

Family-Teachers are carefully screened and thoroughly interviewed before they are hired. Because of the careful selection process, thorough training, and support systems, the vast majority of Family-Teachers enjoy great success in helping youth find healing and hope. More than 50 percent stay at Boys Town two or more years, and 25 percent stay in excess of five years. Some couples, of course, do not make it through the first year of intensive training and evaluation. But those couples who do make it and become certified for the first time stay at Boys Town as Family-Teachers for three years or more. Compared to national figures, the Family-Teachers' length of stay on the job is about three times longer than most child-care workers whose average is only about six to nine months.

Certified Family-Teachers are in demand at Boys Town sites across the nation. Many Boys Town administrators as well as trainers in the Boys Town National Resource and Training Center began as Family-Teachers. An additional number of Family-Teachers who started out at Boys Town have gone on to responsible positions in other human service agencies both public and private.

A Philosophy of Family

Boys Town prides itself on taking kids who have long histories of troubles of every kind (abandonment, abuse, neglect, drugs, alcohol, stealing, delinquency, mental illness) and who have not lived successfully or happily in a family. It should be obvious that sometimes it isn't even their fault. Life has failed them, not at the middle or at the end, but at the very beginning. On average, a youth who comes to our Boys Town Family Home Program finds this to be the third or fourth place they have lived. All who come feel the crying need for success in terms of love, warmth, and stability. Yet far too many feel themselves to be terrible failures in this regard. They even hate school. Why? Because that, too, is a place where failure occurs.

The Family-Teachers' role in responding to their needs is a difficult and demanding one. Remember, the name Family-Teacher means a person who teaches family skills, builds relationships, and empowers youth to take responsibility for their own life, health, education, and well being. So their responsibility is to succeed where others have not and with children who will test their patience, their love, and their talents in every imaginable way time and again. These are children who have grown up amid much instability and anxiety. Before coming to us, they would often awaken in the morning, not knowing whether breakfast or a beating would await them.

Family-Teachers provide a family where these youth can get their physical, emotional, and spiritual needs met in a proactive manner – without resort to drugs or alcohol or suicide ideation of the past. Their job is to provide a family setting with stability and security which alone can communicate effectively to a troubled child that he or she is safe and loved – every day. They work within the context of a family that teaches each child what he or she needs to know to be a happy, confident, caring person. Especially they need to "get to" the child, to help the child "open up," to evoke the child's trust and cooperation. For it is within the family that each child learns the skills, builds the relationships, and finds himself or herself empowered to grow toward spiritual, emotional, and social maturity. No wonder Family-Teachers at Boys Town study hard, work hard, and pray a lot for their kids.

Family-Teachers are there to provide care, concern, love, discipline, and teaching in abundance. They are there to make the meaning of family come alive. They are there to see the kids off to school, talk to their teachers, help them with homework at night, and take their medications. They are there to teach the children to pray and to worship with them as a family. They are there to cheer at the sporting events, cry when things are not going well, and be filled with pride at graduation. Family-Teachers are there to provide special families for special children.

Responsibility, Authority, and Accountability

For a program to be meaningful, it must be lived on a day-to-day basis. For Boys Town's Family Home Program that means that Family-Teachers go about their teaching of family life in three ways:

- Teaching skills
- Building healthy relationships
- Empowering through self-government

They have the primary responsibility for meeting the developmental and treatment needs of each child. They need to help teach children to get in touch with their own feelings, control their impulses, empathize with others, motivate themselves, and delay gratification, all in the context of a loving, caring family.

They need to do this teaching in the midst of managing a household that has six to eight young people living in it. They have the help of professional treatment agents called clinical specialists and clinical supervisors who help solve difficult youth problems, provide advice on home operations, and are always there to lend a hand when needed. In addition, administrative specialists help Family-Teachers with budgets, repairs, and other household business chores.

Responsibility for the well-being of children is a functional concept for Family-Teachers because they have those degrees of authority necessary to do this difficult job. They have the primary responsibility for the children in "their family." This means that Boys Town's Model has turned on its head the usual social service model where primary treatment responsibility rests with "higher-ups" and the line staff simply carry out orders. It is just the opposite at Boys Town. Family-Teachers literally are the primary treatment agents in their homes.

The simplest example is in the area of money management. Most line staff in child care cannot spend five dollars without receiving prior authority. Not so at Boys Town. Family-Teachers really do run their houses and decide how the home's budget is to be spent. They decide what stores to shop in, what groceries to buy, what dry cleaners to use, and even what doctors and dentists to go to from an approved list.

In addition, they make sure the children in their home have a voice in the decisions that affect their lives. Through self-government and Family-Teacher guidance, the kids decide what they will do for recreation, what movies they will see, where they will go, and what activities they will engage in. The more a Boys Town home resembles a normal home, the more chances there are that the youth there will find family warmth and learn the skills necessary to get better and to assume control of their own lives.

In all cases, giving Family-Teachers sufficient authority allows them to effectively and flexibly meet the physical, emotional, social, and spiritual needs of each child.

Of course, with responsibility and authority comes accountability. The accountability systems at Boys Town help answer the most important questions of all:

- How do you know it's working?

- Are kids happy?

- Are they getting better?
- Are they empowered with a voice in decisions about their treatment and life in the home?
- Are they building healthy relationships?
- Is the home cared for and in good repair?
- Is the budget being spent appropriately?
- Are parents, probation officers, and social workers satisfied with the process and outcomes of treatment?
- Are the rest of the staff supportive enough?

Accountability systems at Boys Town have been designed to answer these questions and more. That makes Boys Town a pretty unique place. After the information is collected, it is routinely reported back. Areas that need improvement are given special attention so a good job can be better done in the future. We make every effort here at Boys Town to give negative feedback in a positive way. That permits everyone to recognize what possibilities there are to do our jobs better in a positive, healthy atmosphere. This is a key to quality care.

As you can see, the Boys Town Family Home Program literally means that each home is a family and as such is a very special place indeed.

Where do Family-Teachers come from?

They come from all parts of the country. They hear about these opportunities in many ways, especially from friends, teachers, pastors, social workers, and others. They may have seen an ad somewhere.

On October 3, Tom and Debbie Pierce were hired as Family-Teachers at Boys Town. They had heard first about the job from a cousin who was a Family-Teacher at Boys Town, and when they read an ad in their Sacramento newspaper in August, they immediately called (as the ad advised them to do) and went through a telephone screening interview as did thirteen other couples. They were then among seven couples who were asked to complete the written application forms. On September 10, a Boys Town staff member came to Sacramento to interview these seven couples, and as a result, Tom and Debbie and two other couples were invited to Boys Town, Nebraska, for a final interview. Tom and Debbie were delighted when they were chosen.

What does Boys Town look for in selecting new Family-Teachers?

- **A rock-solid marriage.** This relationship must be solid enough for the couple to work closely together and to share equally in the task for caring for up to six to eight kids who have so many needs. That's a must.

- **Second, they both need natural parenting skills.** That means lots of warmth, patience, good humor, vitality, a way with kids, a strong sense of right and wrong, and a good, solid religious faith. Did I mention patience? I hope so. As Family-Teachers they will need to be good role models for their kids and behave on a day-to-day basis in ways that we would like kids to emulate. They need to be outgoing people who enjoy being with kids.
- **Third, they need to have themselves been successful in school.** We like them to have been successful in college, but as a minimum, a high school education with good life experience would also be acceptable.
- **Fourth, they need to be trainable.** Boys Town's model of care is very specific, and everyone has to learn it. If the two think they already have all the answers and don't need to learn any new ones, then they will not be successful as Family-Teachers at Boys Town and should seek to use their skills elsewhere.

Tom and Debbie seemed to fit Boys Town's selection requirements. Debbie taught sixth grade, and Tom was a salesman for a paper company. They both did volunteer work with youth groups at their church. They both enjoy working with kids and liked the idea of being really in charge of a home (not just line staff) to maximize their influence. While Tom and Debbie were 30 years old and had been married six years, they had no children of their own (sometimes Family-Teachers have one or two children of their own and that is a plus). During the selection interview it became clear that the Pierces had a family style that would be beneficial and fun for the kids.

When they were told they were accepted as Family-Teachers in our Southern California program, it was a time for big hugs all around. They were welcomed into the Boys Town family, and a date was given for them to begin the preservice training in the famous Village of Boys Town in Nebraska. There are lots of reasons for Boys Town concentrating its preservice training for residential care in the Nebraska Village founded by Father Flanagan. It's here where they can most easily catch Father Flanagan's spirit that is still alive and which is a wellspring of energy for all of us. It is also in the Village where they can see sixty-six Boys Town homes all working together for the benefit of children. It is the most unusual Village in the world, and we believe the happiest.

They will be joined in the preservice workshop at Boys Town, Nebraska, by five other Family-Teacher couples together with four

Assistant Family-Teachers who will begin their training also.

Every couple in a Boys Town home has an Assistant Family-Teacher who works side by side with Family-Teachers to assist them with all their duties and responsibilities in teaching youth the skills they need in helping them build relationships and empowering them to take charge of their own lives.

Assistant Family-Teachers tend to be younger, often just out of graduate school or young people who just want to help kids.

What does Boys Town look for in selecting Assistant Family-Teachers?

- **They first need to be team players.** Yes, they need to be people who can work well with a couple, supporting the couple's treatment planning, family style, and warmth. They need to be people who can run the house by themselves as needed (when Family-Teachers are getting some time off), and who can be very much a part of the treatment team, effective, happy, and a good role model.

- **They need natural parenting skills.** That means lots of patience, good humor, vitality, a way with kids, a strong sense of right and wrong, and a good, solid religious faith. Did I mention patience? I hope so. As Assistant

Family-Teachers they will need to be good role models for the kids and behave on a day-to-day basis in ways that we would like kids to emulate. They need to be outgoing people who enjoy being with kids.

- **They need to have themselves been successful in school.** We like them to have been successful in college, but as a minimum, a high school education with good life experience would also be acceptable.
- **They need to be trainable.** Boys Town's Model of care is very specific, and everyone has to learn it. If a person thinks he already has all the answers and doesn't need to learn any new ones, then he will not be successful as an Assistant Family-Teacher at Boys Town and should seek to use his skills elsewhere.

It is Family-Teachers and Assistant Family-Teachers who are dedicated, have natural talents, and have the benefit of Boys Town's training and consultation to make it work.

Family-Style Living

While Family-Teachers and Assistant Family-Teachers are the heart of the program, the other key ingredient to our success is family-style living. Family-style living means having a married couple live in the home with a small number of children. It is their home with their personal touches and their belongings in every room. It must not smell antiseptic like an institution. It must not look like an institution. It must look like a home, act like a home, smell like a home, and be a home – Tom and Debbie's home.

Family-style living means that the couple and the kids function as a family. And don't forget the Assistant, too. They prepare meals together and eat together. They play together. They pray together and go to church together. They make decisions together. They go shopping together. They celebrate birthdays and important occasions together. They work together to help each other and support each other.

Family-style living is very important because most Boys Town kids have not had positive experiences in a family setting. They have not experienced the success or perhaps warmth or cooperation of working with a loving, caring couple. They have not seen a married couple solve problems in a quiet, rational fashion. They have not always been around people who interact with each other in helpful, considerate, and cooperative ways. They have not had the advantages offered by Family-Teachers who help the kids to learn to participate in a family. They have not been taught the skills or helped build relationships or been empowered to get better. In many cases, they have had just the opposite:

abandonment, abuse, neglect, or mental illness.
Or perhaps they just rejected their families.

For kids with few options in life, the family
home really can become a home, a place to even
come back to, a place where they are always
welcome and supported.

Why Family-Teachers?

This is an important question. It is asked
frequently. Usually it is phrased this way: "Why
Family-Teachers? Why not shift staff workers?"
Or, "We tried houseparents and it didn't work."

In our long-term residential programs, Boys
Town uses (as the centerpiece of treatment)
neither shift staff nor houseparents. We even
invented the name Family-Teachers because they
"teach family." They are uniquely the principal
treatment agents for children to learn family
skills, family relationships, family values, and
self-discipline.

Family-Teachers have a good number of
responsibilities that shift staff workers and
houseparents so often do not have. They live in
the home and provide treatment for up to eight
children. This is not like shift staff workers who
work for eight hours and go home. Shift staff
workers are wonderful people. Often they
provide care but treatment is done by social
workers, psychologists, psychiatrists, or others
outside the living environment. So, why
Family-Teachers?

First of all, live-in married couples help create family-style living. Houseparents could do that too, and there are many wonderful houseparents in our country. But they are not highly trained professionals who have the specific know-how to teach the skills and build the relationships and empower our children (who have such serious problems) in accordance with their needs. The Family-Teachers live in the home with the kids. It is their home. It is not just a place to work for a few hours each day. So, for example, Thanksgiving Day with all its warmth, including a big dinner, is celebrated "at home." No wonder kids love it so much.

Second, Family-Teachers promote the development of positive, healthy relationships between themselves and the youngsters. By living together, day after day, the kids and the couple grow to know each other very well and develop lasting friendships.

Third, communication is made easier for treatment purposes. Since the Family-Teachers are there all the time, they know what Joey did last night and also what he did this morning. The Family-Teachers can help Joey all day, every day, even with subtle problems that occur only once in a while. It is easier to fool a shift staff worker who doesn't know what happened on the other two shifts in the home. It's pretty hard to fool a Family-Teacher.

Fourth, accountability for the progress of the kids and the operation of the home is easier to assign. When Joey is making progress, the couple gets credit. If Joey is not making progress, the couple gets the clinical help they need in order to reverse this – because it is easy to determine who is responsible for teaching Joey how to problem solve when feeling depressed, how to control his impulses when very angry, and how to gain self mastery. It is much easier to provide the help and advice needed so Joey can learn to take charge of his own life. Time does not have to be spent trying to determine which shift staff person needs what kind of assistance or where communication is breaking down between them.

Fifth, married couples can best provide appropriate models for faith, morality, and family life. As a married couple, they show how family life can be lived by working together, praying together, problem solving together, and making a life together. Married couples assume a unique role in teaching. They role model what good spouses look like. Many children have never seen such healthy role models. A boy, for example, needs to apprentice himself to a man who can teach him what it means to be both a husband and a father. A boy is a true apprentice. He learns all kinds of how-to things. And at the same time, he builds a mature relationship with an adult male. If a father teaches his son to fish, he has not just taught him the skill of fishing, he has built a relationship with his son. Just as a boy learns certain things from an adult male about being a husband and father, he also learns from his female Family-Teacher what it means to be a successful wife and mother. They both teach skills and help build the healthy relationships that a boy desperately needs. So, too, with our girls.

Sixth, Family-Teachers together with their youth provide excellent care for the home, the van, the furniture, the kitchen, and even the yard and garden. It is *their* home. It is where they live with the kids. The more it is their home, the more warmth it has. It is more than a place to go to work. Now you can see why we say Family-Teachers have more responsibility than shift staff workers. It is not surprising then that Family-Teachers and their Assistants not only tend to take better care of their home, they also make it look and feel more homelike. Family-Teachers are likelier to make events more fun, meals more tasty, birthdays more important, Sunday church services more personal, and outings more a part of normal life.

Administrators like the Family-Teacher system for another reason centering on staff turnover. Usually when houseparents leave a home, "their program" goes with them and when new houseparents come, "their program" is often different from the old houseparents' program. That is not so with the Family-Teacher system. All are trained in the same Boys Town treatment methods, and all put those methods into practice. Continuity of program is not a problem when you use Family-Teachers.

With Family-Teachers there is both a strong family atmosphere (lacking in shift staff facilities) and strong program continuity during staff transitions (a problem when houseparents leave). This is because the Family Home Program remains in place in the home – as does the Assistant Family-Teacher – even though a new couple, who is early in their training sequence, is now operating the program. The new couple may not be as sophisticated as the experienced couple who left, but their training has prepared them to be good professionals, operating the same treatment program in a warm, family environment. That is so very important.

With Family-Teachers providing care and treatment with and for each youngster each day, strong personal relationships can be developed and sustained. This is a tremendous benefit to kids who often have not had a positive relationship with any adult. The intense working contacts with Family-Teachers provide an opportunity for the relationship to form, be nurtured, and grow strong.

But this advantage is also a disadvantage when one couple leaves and a new couple moves into the home. Turnover in Family-Teachers is often a more personal and traumatic event compared to turnover of shift staff workers. In our experience, however, the benefit of a Family-Teacher couple to children more often than not outweighs the transition.

Family-Teachers are not houseparents nor are they shift staff workers. They are carefully selected, highly trained professionals. They truly are special people doing a special job, and that's why Boys Town has Family-Teachers.

Assistant Family-Teachers are also carefully selected, highly trained professionals. They, too, are special people doing a special job as part of the team. That is why Boys Town has Assistant Family-Teachers.

Chapter 3

A Day in the Life of a Family-Teacher

A Family-Teacher's life is so unique and so challenging, I thought it would be fun for you to walk through one day in their shoes.

Please remember, Father Flanagan popularized the idea "there is no such thing as a bad boy or a bad girl." The kids that come to us are hurt. They are sometimes very ill. And they have developed lots of behaviors that are hurtful to themselves and hurtful to others. Every day at Boys Town is a good day to bring healing and hope to these troubled children who come from every family stratum in America and every state in the Union.

The couple, Ray and Julie, who will share with you in this chapter, are one of many Family-Teacher couples who devote their lives to helping our children. They believe, just as I believe, that if you have a lot of love, a lot of affection, if you have deep religious faith, and if you develop the skills that are necessary, you can actually help these children change their behavior and put joy back in their hearts. We believe there is always room for hope. I hope you do, too. So let's see another day begin to unfold at Boys Town. Listen to Ray and Julie.

Ray: Right now we have seven young men in our home. They range from 14 to 18 right now. We've been Family-Teachers for about two and a half years. The first four months when we got here, we were in transition where you kind of substitute and go into other homes and see how their programs run. It's a time to learn so much.

Julie: And then we moved into our home about two years ago. I think the main thing I like about the Boys Town Model is that the kids get to see what a normal, everyday family is like. They get to see Ray and me in a normal marriage relationship. They get to see Ray, me, and our little Christine in a normal family relationship. And by watching and taking part in a real family, hopefully our boys begin to form an idea of what they should grow up in when they have a family and when they have a wife. How they should treat their spouse or their children. So hopefully we can make them feel as comfortable as we possibly can and make them feel part of our family.

Ray: This much by itself can give them some of the basic skills they need to succeed when they leave. Of course, their treatment needs are immense, and Julie and I are the primary treatment agents in their lives, giving healing and hope. I think that's our ultimate goal – to give them the best opportunity to be a successful person.

Julie: We have one daughter. She is 22 months old. And we're expecting our next child October 2nd.

Ray: I definitely feel it's an advantage to have natural children in your home. It brings a little bit of unity with the other kids. You can also role-model how you parent them. It shows the kids what you would normally do with your own children, and it helps bring things together – like with family outings. They see younger kids involved with some of the things we do.

Julie: When we first moved into the home, I was pregnant with Christine, and I think that that's one of the main things that helped bring our home together as a real family was the guys seeing Christine and seeing us with our natural children. Being involved in that process was a really neat thing for the guys because a lot of them had never been around a small child before.

Ray: Last night we all went to the football game to watch Reggie play. It was a beautiful fall night, and Reggie did a nice job scoring a touchdown. We had a good time, and the kids' behavior was very appropriate.

Julie: And yesterday morning while the kids were in school, we had our weekly meeting with our clinical specialist. At that time we sit down at the kitchen table and review the progress of all of our guys and how they are doing through that week. There are treatment issues for each. It's so important for their getting better.

Ray: The clinical meeting is a great support system. It's a time for us to discuss things with our specialist that we need help with and even things we feel maybe we're not getting supported on. Sometimes we are stymied with a youth not getting better, and our specialist is always there to help out.

Julie: Before a Family-Teacher couple is ever placed in a home, we go through a three-week preservice training process. It's a very intense training program, involving interactive video and role plays where we get the experience of actually dealing with children in a situation. Trainees are videotaped, so we get a chance to do the behaviors ourselves before a camera to see how we have picked up the skills. Once we have completed that three-week training process, then we usually go into the transition phase, and then we move into our own home. At that point the training is taken over by the clinical specialist in our home. This includes treatment planning and ongoing training, providing feedback to us, commenting on our style of interacting, our relationships with the children, and so on. There are also advanced workshops that we need to attend. Part of the fun of being a Family-Teacher is that you are constantly learning more and more how to help your kids.

Ray: Paperwork is necessary in almost every job, but it helps to keep us accountable for what we are doing, and it's kind of like a system of checks and balances. We spent the early part of Friday afternoon (before the kids came home) working on reports with our administrative specialist who helps with budgets and repairs. When our youth come home from school, around 3 p.m., they each go over their day with us. All the kids are sent to school with a card which every teacher signs off on each class period: Did the youth do his homework? Was his behavior and attitude good? Did he take an active part in class? We go through the card, period by period, and go through what behaviors they displayed, and we have them give us a little bit more detail about what they've done. There's a lot of praising that goes on here. Our kids soon learn school is a place of success, not failure. No wonder they like it.

Julie: Our Assistant Family-Teacher, John, comes on duty at 2:30 p.m. and will stay until the kids are in bed. John's main job is to help out the Family-Teachers, and John does such a good job. He also helps us run errands that we need to run or takes our kids to doctor's appointments. He also helps teach skills and is a vital member of the treatment team. And Monday, when Ray and I are taking time off, John will be here and run the house in our absence.

Ray: We spend a lot of time working with our youth about many different issues. Sometimes kids want to hurt themselves or feel like running away. We sit down and do some problem solving with them, showing them that there are always positive options to choose from.

Julie: We teach them the importance of religion. When they first arrive, most of our kids are powerless before the forces of abuse and neglect, anger and violence of their lives. If you're powerless, you can't get better unless you get in touch with a Higher Power. So religion is necessary for getting better. It is not optional. That's why Family-Teachers and Assistant Family-Teachers need to have a faith life themselves. You can't teach what you don't live yourself. Ray and I share our faith with our kids.

Ray: Also our schools are very helpful in providing religious instruction. They teach our kids a lot of the basics. By having the school and the home working together, especially in the area of morality, it creates a real nice blend of teaching. And we can follow up on their teaching and integrate it into our treatment planning. For example, doing drugs isn't just a matter of chemicals coursing through a kid's veins. It's a lifestyle. If you want to quit drugs, you have to quit looking like a druggie, dressing like a druggie, talking like a druggie, and acting like a druggie.

Julie: I believe a good home has good meals. The kids help plan our menus. And each one takes a turn cooking supper. This is a little chaotic at first (our boys come with almost no idea of how to make a tasty meal). But it's worth the effort. We'll usually take two or three kids with us for grocery shopping. We often do some comparison shopping, asking them to look at the price to see which would be a better buy.

Ray: We want them to learn how to fix nutritional meals. We also want them to learn how to take care of their self-care maintenance, personal hygiene, personal appearance. Many have never been taught. And not a few come with problems of enuresis and encopresis. They feel so much better when they learn to be neat and clean and well groomed. We also want to make sure they know how to maintain a clean house.

Julie: We eat supper usually around 5:30. We never let a meal start without a prayer of thanks to the Lord for His blessings. Mealtime is a great time to practice our conversation skills. Someone once said: Teenagers are "deaf and dumb" at the family dinner table. But just the opposite is true at Boys Town.

Ray: We often start with just the basic table skills. Our young men come with deficits. We start right from point one. You put your napkin in your lap. Some kids don't even know how to use a knife or fork. Again, it may sound really elementary, but a lot of the things that we take for granted, these young men were never taught. Many kids don't have those rudimentary social graces. Remember: our model is a teaching model. When they leave Boys Town for their first job interview or when they are first put in a spot where they are in the public, we want them to feel very, very comfortable.

Julie: We have a few young men currently involved in football and we have two on the varsity football team. We're proud of them.

Ray: One is a sophomore and got a chance to play varsity so that was quite an accomplishment for him and really made our home just as proud. The guys in the home remarked at how that was an accomplishment.

Julie: Every night after dinner, we have a family conference. It normally happens at the dinner table. We had a short one last night because of the football game. And the process itself is intended for the young men to take an active part in their own treatment. Kids who are actively involved in their own treatment get better faster than kids who passively comply with treatment strategies.

Ray: They don't see Julie and myself and John, our Assistant, as being too controlling because they know that this is an area of home life they really do participate in. We call it our self-government system. They often think of it as times when they have concerns or when they feel like they want to change something, that we can all meet together and their voice is heard. We think of it as much more treatment-oriented. Both are important. So they look forward to that nightly family conference. It's also a useful tool that we can use to have them see us as being very fair. You know, we're not always making the rules and decisions. We give them an opportunity to use good skills, do rational problem solving, and come up with answers to problems themselves.

Julie: The bottom line is that Family-Teaching is not just a job. It's our lifestyle. We live Family-Teaching. We enjoy working here. Probably the biggest joy for both of us, at least for me, is to be able to see the progress that we have made with our kids. Sometimes it's just a little bit of progress, but it is progress. I mean we work at the best child-care facility in the world. And the programs and the training and the tools that we have to help these kids are the best, and they work. It honestly works.

Ray: We've seen some kids who when we first started were real tough kids to work with. We put a lot of time and effort into the kids, but the progress that we've seen now is so worth it. It means so much to your heart to see these kids just change and grow and mature and become a lot more responsible. You know that they are more successful by the things that they have already accomplished. That makes some of the bad days worthwhile. It counts for a lot.

Julie: I guess one of the best things about this job is that there is never a dull moment. You will probably never, ever face job boredom or boredom within your home because there is always something to do. There's always something new going on with your youth in the home, something that you can learn from, that you can find new ways in which to teach. It's exciting. It keeps you busy. It keeps you hopping.

Ray: I think you are always learning. You are able to apply the technology that is learned through Boys Town, and they give you quite a big toolbox. You help kids get so much better that when they walk across the stage to get their diploma, you feel so happy, so proud. You feel energized. And through the years they come back again, each time with a greater understanding of what Julie and I have done and a greater gratitude for what the whole Boys Town experience has been for them.

Four Child-Care Technologies

As we come to the end of this chapter, let us look at what lies ahead. To understand what is so special about Boys Town, we also need to look at the basic technologies or building blocks of the Family-Teacher system at Boys Town, namely:

1. Training

2. Consultation

3. Evaluation

4. Administration

These are so critically important to Boys Town's success in helping kids that we need to devote a special chapter to each of them. We will take them one by one.

Chapter 4

Training

*T*he word "training" means something very specific at Boys Town. It is a set of proven technologies used to help our kids produce positive, beneficial changes in their lives. It is the first of four vital components which all staff must constantly enrich their professional lives with, if we are to be successful with our Boys Town children and families.

What is it all about?

You might think that Boys Town training would be sort of like some university courses where social workers learn very valuable theories and techniques for dealing with state child welfare agencies or other professionals. It is not.

You might think it would be lots of hours spent learning how the staff in this particular agency works, what forms to fill out, what permissions to ask for, what kids are allowed to do. It is not.

What is it all about? Let's start with some stories:

Lisa is 14 years old and is from Long Beach. She saw her father kill her mother with a butcher knife in a most brutal fashion. That was five years ago. Since then she has failed at school, lost hope in life, has tried to hurt herself many times, and been in and out of mental health programs. She feels her life is not worth living.

Then there is Joe. Joe is from the South Bronx in New York. His mother is a prostitute and a drug addict who sells herself for money. His sister is also on drugs and has been in pornographic films. His mother introduced him to marijuana and said it would be good for him and would calm him down.

John, age 14, has had eleven prior placements before coming to Boys Town – all in the last four years. He runs away frequently. That's how he got eleven placements before he arrived here.

Here is George, age 11, with cigarette burns on his arms when he came to Boys Town. His mother used burning cigarettes to punish him for behaviors she did not like. She is mentally ill.

Then there is Tom, age 13. He was chained to a bed by his father for the last six years when he wasn't in school and was beaten on a regular basis.

Here is Mary, age 16, sexually abused by her father and uncle since the age of 8. She is extremely promiscuous. She feels rotten about herself. She does not know how to seek affection except in ways that will punish her and make her feel cheap and lousy about herself.

Then there is Laura. She was sexually abused by her mother's boyfriend at age 6. She was raped when she was 11. At 12, she was admitted to Boys Town.

Here is Sam. His mother and father are pretty much like most moms and dads today. They are hard working and successfully raised Sam's three older brothers. Why Sam is so truant and mixed up in drugs and shoplifting is a mystery to them.

And then there is Maria. She has been in and out of psychiatric hospitals many times, diagnosed as bi-polar. She has found little success in school or any place else. We are her last and only hope.

These are kids with problems, lots of problems. They have been through a lot already in their young lives. They have been abandoned, abused, neglected, or simply alienated from others. They cannot make it at home, in school, or in the community. That is why they come to a Boys Town program.

A Positive Approach

These kids have already seen the negative side of life. At all Boys Town sites across America, everything is set up to have them experience the positive side of things. Even discipline is carried out positively to help each youngster learn new ways of dealing with life. This is not easy to do.

It takes a lot of hard work to help kids learn how to deal with so many problems. It takes deep religious motivation to work day after day successfully with these youngsters. It takes a series of treatment technologies that are effective. It takes planning and precision in the use of these treatment modalities to help the kids progress toward their goals of healing and hope.

That is why Boys Town provides a unique and extensive system of training to each staff member including Family-Teachers and Assistant Family-Teachers. At Boys Town, training starts before a couple or an Assistant moves into a home and never stops as long as they work at Boys Town. Training is an ongoing process, and it begins with the Preservice Workshop. Before describing the workshop itself, let's look at what is being trained in the 21st century Boys Town Teaching Model.

As we said earlier, the Boys Town Teaching Model was developed more than three decades ago, starting at Kansas University in a small setting and then taking root and being adapted to a larger homelike setting in the Village of Boys Town, Nebraska.

After significant success there, Boys Town developed a way of transferring this technology to short-term residential facilities (shelters), parent training, in-home services, treatment foster care, schools, and psychiatric hospitals.

So whatever else happens in training, each Family-Teacher and Assistant Family-Teacher will have to be trained in this Model. Let's first call to mind what the Model is like, especially in its 21st century form. This is one clear way to explain why those who use it need to be "teachable."

1. **There are four characteristics of the Boys Town Model of care:**
   - **It is safe.** So often our kids have come from places that are not safe. Above all, we must create a safe place with a safe program.
   - **The Model is effective.** That means that kids really get better. Remember, Lisa can't get better in dealing with suicide ideation until she starts learning problem-solving skills. Suicide is a long-term solution to a short-term problem. Learning problem-solving skills is as good a place as any to start. (With each one of the stories of the kids mentioned above, there is a specific set of behavioral skills that need to be learned as a starting place for getting better. We have to assure when children come here that they do get better.)
   - **The Model is humane.** This simply means that we don't just have technology but that we also treat kids with love and respect. It means that kids should like the Boys Town program they are in. They should feel good about it. Children can't motivate themselves

to get better if they don't like it here. They
need to be treated with respect. Or, to use
the words of the streets, for kids to like it
here Family-Teachers need to learn how to
put into effect two basic rules:

a) We won't "diss" our kids or let others
"diss" them either.

b) We won't let a youth "diss" anybody
else, peers or staff.

- **It is replicable.** That means that you and I
and so many others across America can be
taught to use it.

2. The Boys Town Model is:

- **Family-centered.** It is clear from what we
said that Boys Town's long-term care is
family-centered. In an analogous way as far
as possible, we want our shelters to feel like
a family place. We want our parent training
to be family-oriented. We want our foster
care to feel like a family. We want our in-
home services to make the family stronger.
We want our school services to convince
administrators that a school should have a
family atmosphere. And we want hospital
administrators to understand that children
will get better far faster in psychiatric
hospitals if they feel more like a family.

- **Outcome-oriented.** That means that we
don't judge success on the basis of how

many hours children spent in school or how many hours of therapy they received. But we judge school success on what they learned and what their grades are. In other words, are they doing better in school? And we judge therapeutic success on what skills they learned through therapy and whether they are applying those skills at Boys Town and elsewhere. The question is: Are they getting better, feeling better, acting better?

- **Research-based.** This is a very important point. We first helped develop this Model in the 1970s because we couldn't help kids get better with the old techniques we had been using. We had kids come to us with problems of abuse of every kind, neglect, drugs, and alcohol, and no therapies at the time really worked very well with our kind of kids. They really didn't help our kids get better. We never thought in those days that once we developed the Model we would have to keep doing research because the problems of children would change. But the problems have changed in the 1980s and 1990s, continuing to get worse, and that's why we need to continue to research new and better ways of dealing with the youth and family problems of the 21st century.

3. **The Model teaches Family-Teachers and all staff how to help kids find healing and hope in three very specific concrete ways:**
   - **How to teach skills.** There are some skills that every youth needs to learn to be successful. And then there are specific skills for specific problem areas.
   - **How to build healthy relationships.** To learn how to build healthy relationships is quite different from learning how to teach skills. There is a set of technologies here as well.
   - **How to empower through self-government.** Study after study shows that kids get better faster if they have a voice in the decisions that affect their lives. This is what self-government is all about. Remember, it has nothing to do with "letting the kids get away with whatever they want to." Self-government means insisting that boys and girls take an active part in how they learn skills, how they develop relationships, and how they discover healing and hope.

4. **This is a self-help model.** Families need to learn self-help strategies. Our goal is not to control young people but to help them learn to take charge of their own lives, learning self-

discipline and self-control. So the goals of our treatment of children include:

- Self-fulfillment
- Self-expression
- Self-talk
- Self-respect
- Self-image
- Self-esteem
- Self-direction

5. **This is a family model.** So we have to help boys and girls learn:
   - How to be a son or daughter
   - How to be a brother or sister
   - How to be a husband and father
   - How to be a wife and mother
   - How to be successful in family life

6. **It is a teaching model.** We teach kids to stop, think, and choose. It is not a counseling model, though it includes counseling. It is not a group interaction model, although it incorporates elements of group interaction. It is not a punishment model, although "we won't let you get away with anything." We believe that kids come to us because they lack skills, and it is our responsibility to teach them. Punishment does not do that with these kids.

It is not a control model. We don't expect blind obedience from our kids. Empowerment and self-government – allowing children to have a voice in decisions that affect their lives – are essential. So the Boys Town Model teaches empowerment, relationship-building, and self-government.

7. **The Model teaches a person how to develop the ability to:**
   - **Monitor one's feelings.** Because of abuse or neglect, many of our kids are unable to express their feelings or even figure out what they mean. This is an important area of learning.
   - **Control impulses.** They are angry at life. If you're so angry in life that you lash out, impulse control isn't a luxury. It's a necessity.
   - **Empathize with others.** Sometimes we have been so hurt that we just engage in self-pity and do not learn to empathize with others. And if we have been hurt badly enough, sometimes we become so pathological that we enjoy hurting others instead of empathizing with them.
   - **Delay gratification.** Education is basic experience in delaying gratification. There is an old saying: "Knowledge maketh a bloody entry." You only feel good when you get a good grade on the test and when you apply what you learned. Then you feel terrific. But there is a delay between the learning and the feeling terrific.

In summary, the Model has integrated cognitive and affective elements (thinking and feeling) with behavior.

Generalization in this new version of the Model is at the front, not at the back, of the process. Most models (including versions of the medical model, the positive peer culture model, and the old behavioral model) put generalization at the end. They train kids and hope the kids continue to use these skills after they leave the program.

A characteristic of this Model is moving beyond the "train-and-hope" way of thinking by teaching self-discipline skills from the start. This enables youth to not only practice them from the beginning, but also to begin to understand that: "If I learn self-control under these circumstances, I'll be a happier person because I can practice self-control wherever I go." Simply stated, the Teaching Model teaches generalization.

Another characteristic is internalization. One criticism of old style behaviorism (disregarding a person's thoughts and feelings) was its inattention to internalization. In other words, "Control the environment, and don't worry about anything else." That description may be a stereotype, but there is a great deal of accuracy in how often it worked out that way in practice. Our Teaching Model focuses on internalization, integrating feelings, thoughts, and behavior.

The essence of the Model is teaching skills, building relationships, and empowerment. From the beginning, our staff members learn how to accomplish these tasks.

We start with the family, which is the source of all human fulfillment. The family is where teaching skills and building relationships are most visibly and compassionately intertwined. The family is the source of a person's identity and sense of community. Teaching skills and building relationships are not independent but rather dependent on each other. For example, if a father teaches his daughter how to shoot a basket, he has not just taught her the skill of basketball, he has built a relationship with his daughter.

This is what Preservice Workshop is all about. Our Family-Teachers and Assistants, shelter workers, in-home service workers, parent trainers, school trainers, hospital trainers all need to learn how to impart these skills.

Preservice Workshop

The Preservice Workshop is the first experience of Boys Town training. It occurs prior to a couple operating a home and prior to anyone working with kids. The Preservice Workshop teaches couples the central skills they will need.

Family-Teachers and all those in training quickly learn there are three types of teaching:

- **Proactive teaching**, which is simply teaching skills at a neutral time.
- **Corrective teaching**, which is quite different. It is problem-time teaching. We need to teach people to help youngsters when there is a problem, to problem solve and move on.
- **Crisis teaching**, which is simply corrective teaching with youth who are upset and very angry and out of self-control.

Each has its own set of things to accomplish, yet all three are based on the same foundation of the Model.

This Preservice Workshop is three weeks in length. About 50 percent of the time is spent role playing or practicing the skills that will be needed when operating their home or other program. For example, adult trainers play the role of an agitated "youth" while trainees help the "youth" by putting lecture materials into practice. With the role-playing method, the staff member can quickly discover which skills he or she has mastered and which skills are yet unrefined before having to apply them with a youth.

Let's take a brief look at the Preservice Workshop schedule. You can see that training is a very busy time for everyone.

Boys Town Preservice Training Schedule

First Week

Monday

9:30 a.m. - 1:00 p.m.	New Employee Orientation

Tuesday

8:30 - 10:30 a.m.	Welcome/Overview
10:30 a.m. - Noon	History of Boys Town and Boys Town USA
1:00 - 2:30 p.m.	Professionalism
2:45 - 4:30 p.m.	Clinical Implications of Learning and Developmental Theory

Wednesday

8:30 a.m. - Noon	Observing and Describing/ Group Activity
1:00 - 2:45 p.m.	Relationship Building
3:00 - 4:30 p.m.	Effective Praise/Role Play

Thursday

8:30 - 9:00 a.m.	Review
9:00 a.m. - Noon	Daily Points/Empowerment Conference
1:00 - 3:00 p.m.	Weekly Points

Friday

8:30 - 9:30 a.m.	Achievement
9:45 - 11:45 a.m.	Subsystems
1:00 - 3:30 p.m.	Proactive Teaching/Role Play

Second Week

Monday

8:30 - 9:15 a.m.	Auctions
9:30 a.m. - Noon	Corrective Teaching/ Role Play
1:00 - 3:00 p.m.	Sexual Abuse
3:00 - 4:30 p.m.	Youth Rights

Tuesday

8:30 a.m. - Noon	Crisis Teaching Procedures
1:00 - 4:30 p.m.	Crisis Teaching/Role Play

Wednesday

8:30 - 11:30 a.m.	Safety Techniques for Aggressive Behavior
12:30 - 4:30 p.m.	Understanding Diversity

Thursday

8:30 -9:00 a.m.	Reporting Systems
9:15 - 10:00 a.m.	Manager System
10:15 - 11:45 a.m.	Family Meeting
1:00 - 4:00 p.m.	Problem Solving/Role Play
5:30 - 7:00 p.m.	Practicums (Dinner in a Family Home)

Friday

8:30 - 10:00 a.m.	Safety of Children in the Home
10:00 a.m. - Noon	Home Operations
1:00 - 2:15 p.m.	Emergency Procedures
2:15 - 3:30 p.m.	Police Issues
3:45 - 4:15 p.m.	Chemical Dependency

Third Week

Monday

8:30 - 10:00 a.m.	Decision Making and Judgment
10:00 a.m. - Noon	Tolerances
1:00 - 2:15 p.m.	Medication Training
2:30 - 4:30 p.m.	Medication Overview

Tuesday

8:30 - 9:30 a.m.	Boys Town Schools/ Community Schools
9:45 - 11:00 a.m.	Interpreting School Cards
1:00 - 3:00 p.m.	Religion at Boys Town
3:15 - 4:15 p.m.	Tour of Chapels

Wednesday

8:30 - 11:00 a.m.	Treatment Planning
11:00 a.m. - Noon	Nutrition
1:00 - 2:15 p.m.	Driving Review
2:15 - 4:30 p.m.	Driving Tutorials/ Individualized Review

Thursday

8:30 - 10:30 a.m.	Suicide
10:30 a.m. - Noon	Transition into the Home
1:00 - 3:00 p.m.	Role Play Review
3:00 p.m.	Graduation/Certificates

The Preservice Workshop is a good time for all our trainees to have their own questions answered. This was important to Sherry and Marvin James when they went through the workshop a year and a half ago. The Jameses had a baby of their own but no experience in working with or living with adolescents who have problems. Sherry and Marvin were in their late 20s and had been married for two years. Both had graduated from a junior college.

Sherry had been a retail sales clerk, and Marvin had been assistant manager at a fast food restaurant. They have one child. They liked the idea of working together as Family-Teachers and sharing responsibility for their baby. They also came to the conclusion that they wanted to give more of their lives to helping others. They have a deep faith in God. They applied for the job of Family-Teacher after they attended a Boys Town workshop on aggression in Baltimore. And they were justifiably proud of the fact that they were chosen to be Family-Teachers.

When Marvin and Sherry went through the preservice training, they did not know yet why Boys Town focuses so much attention on teaching skills to youth. They were also puzzled by the fact that Boys Town would go to so much trouble to set up a structured motivation system when the goal is to get rid of it and have the youngsters do things out of self-control and self-discipline. These were important questions for Marvin and Sherry and good topics for discussion at the Preservice Workshop.

Why set up a structured motivation system and then get rid of it? The Director of Training, Janice Johnson, explained that the kids who come to Boys Town find it very difficult to change. They have learned to survive in a hostile environment by being aggressive or being withdrawn or manipulating people or situations. That is how they manage the pain and suffering in their lives. Upon their arrival here they often see Boys Town as just another place that will try to change them and another place that will surely fail. The Family-Teachers and Assistants need a positive method to get the attention of these youngsters, to help them learn some new healthy ways of interacting with people, and then to let the youngsters experience the positive benefits and outcomes of their new behavior.

This is what the structured motivation system does. It gives the kids an external reason for doing things differently until they realize how good the benefits are and internalize the behavior. It allows the Family-Teachers to be positive and supportive of new, appropriate behavior. As youngsters learn new ways to feel better about themselves and their motivation to become better persons grows, the structure of the motivation system can be faded out. This is a mighty important step. Why? Because we are trying to teach self-control and self-discipline. We're trying to help youngsters take charge of their own lives. It is also a good sign that Family-Teachers are teaching the youngsters the multitude of new behaviors and attitudes needed to get along with others and preparing for a rewarding life as an adult.

The structured motivation system is like a plaster cast physicians use to help heal a broken leg. It is very important to the healing process, and its removal is a good sign that progress is being made.

Why focus on living skills? Because the kids at Boys Town are so lacking in them, and they are so necessary to live happy, productive lives. They not only have living skill deficits related to their problems, they also have deficits due to delays in normal development as adolescents. They have not had the family, educational, or community support necessary for them to learn to be competent adolescents or adults. They are behind, and it is up to Boys Town to help them catch up. It is up to the Jameses and other Family-Teachers to teach the youngsters dozens of living skills slowly but surely every day, starting with skills specific to their treatment, to their reasons for coming to Boys Town. In addition, kids will learn a whole curriculum of basic skills such as following instructions, accepting feedback, and greeting skills, advanced skills such as rational problem solving, and developmental skills such as making friends. Because the kids have so much to learn, the Family-Teachers must teach constantly.

The idea of a curriculum of living skills really came home for the Jameses when they developed their first treatment plan for Kim, a new girl who had problems with stealing. The Jameses and their clinical specialist sat down and reviewed Kim's files. Since she was 8, she had lived with her elderly grandmother. Kim had fair grades in elementary school but poor grades in junior high with a record of poor attendance and suspensions for vandalism, fights, and various disruptions at school. During the same period, she began a series of encounters with the police and the juvenile court for fighting, shoplifting, and breaking into small businesses, stealing clothes, television sets, radios, and the like. Kim had been placed in three foster homes, but none of them had worked out. It was then that Kim came to Boys Town. Things were not going well for Kim at home, in school, or in her community. The judge said to her: "Kim, either succeed at Boys Town or go to lockup."

The Jameses and their clinical specialist decided one focus of their treatment efforts should be on stealing. This was clearly a serious problem that could result in Kim's placement in a more restrictive setting, yet the problem was not solved. In addition, how could you have a family home when someone was stealing from you all the time? Marvin and Sherry developed Kim's treatment plan for stealing. They sat down with Kim and discussed in detail each item in the treatment plan and reviewed how Sherry and Marvin planned to help Kim achieve these goals. They began with what motivated Kim to steal.

The treatment plan for Kim helped to clarify the idea of a living skills curriculum for Marvin and Sherry. The treatment plan was not designed so much to punish stealing as to teach Kim how to be honest and trustworthy and not to steal at all. Trustworthiness, keeping commitments, being a family member, having possessions, good academic behaviors, and money management could be worked on every day. They were all useful skills that Kim needed to know even after she stopped stealing. Kim had to learn to quit using her past as an explanation for her life and a reason to "get even" by stealing. She had to start "honoring her struggle." In essence, the curriculum of living skills is a course of study on how to become a competent, caring, happy, and morally upright adolescent and adult.

Consultation

In the next chapter, we are going to look at something called clinical consultation. It is the second of four major sets of technologies of the Boys Town Model. Clinical consultation begins immediately after one finishes the Preservice Workshop. It continues throughout one's tenure at Boys Town in whatever setting one finds oneself dealing directly with youth. I'm sure you can understand why we consider this consultation to be an integral part of the ongoing training process for helping kids find healing and hope. It, too, helps make Boys Town the special place it is.

Chapter 5

Clinical Consultation

*C*linical consultation is a necessary and continuing part of the professional development of the role of Family-Teachers, Assistant Family-Teachers, and all staff who work directly with children. It has twin goals. On one hand it is a structured way of ongoing learning. On the other hand it is a way to insure that our kids really do get better. These are two sides of the same coin. Continued learning is not a luxury at Boys Town. It is absolutely essential. Without it, we will make the mistake of applying the solutions of the past to the present.

Change occurs so rapidly in the problems of young people that what you learned four or five years ago may simply not be adequate to handle the troubled youth who are in your care today. So the clinical specialist is there to provide a higher level of professional advice on treatment, to help during crises, to provide continuing in-service training, to observe your work, and to be a supporting and understanding friend.

So it is easy to see that consultation services are a necessary and continuing part of the professional development of both new and experienced Family-Teachers at our Boys Town sites across America.

Because of the critical role of the clinical specialist, each of them must become an expert in the Boys Town family program and must be especially prepared for his or her duties and responsibilities.

Chris Jenkins is a clinical specialist for three homes. She was an Assistant Family-Teacher for many years before she moved up the career ladder to her new job. She's a gem.

As clinical specialist, Chris needs to master a whole area of treatment planning under the tutelage of her clinical director.

Her training as a specialist began by her participation in the Boys Town skill-based consultation workshop, followed by an apprentice period with her clinical director, Janice Smith. Janice is there to help Chris develop her skills, to promote her continued growth as a professional, and to oversee the certification process which she needs to achieve.

One helpful way to understand her work is to list the clinical management skills that the specialist helps to inculcate and promote with Family-Teachers and Assistant Family-Teachers in the homes assigned to her:

Transcendental Clinical Services for Each Youth

1. Motivation management skills
Are kids motivated to get better?

2. Self-government skills
Are kids impacting their own treatment?
Are kids reinforced for good decision making?

3. Counseling skills
Are children learning to control themselves?
Are kids learning how to express their feelings?

4. Relationship-building skills
Are kids learning to develop relationships with peers and with their Family-Teachers?
Do children advocate for each other, for their family, for the couple?
Is the couple liked and respected by the kids?

5. Family-style life-giving skills
Is this a place where you would want your child to live?
What does the home feel like?

6. Outcome skills
Is this child getting better?
Are the other children getting better?

Technical Services for Family-Teachers, Assistants, and Other Staff

1. Professional skills

Is the couple getting better at their job?
Have they adapted to their role?
How do they represent their profession?
Are they growing or stagnating?

2. Consumer relations

Are they other-centered or self-centered?
Do they reinforce others they work with?

3. Teaching skills

Are the kids responding to this couple?
How would you react to their teaching?

4. Relationship skills

Is there warmth in their relationship with
   the kids?
Is religious motivation apparent and important?

5. Treatment-planning skills

Do they recognize progress?
Are they learning to be better treatment
   providers?
Are they promoting growth in their children?
Are they asking for help in cases where
   treatment planning is not working well?

To help make the transition a smooth one
when a new Family-Teacher couple takes over,
the clinical specialist carefully guides activities in

the two weeks prior to them moving into their family home. Clinical specialists, the departing Family-Teachers, and the new Family-Teachers meet to review each child's treatment plan, progress, and needs. These needs are not simply technical needs, they are also needs for warmth, caring, sharing, and love.

To paint the picture with a broad stroke, the new couple needs to make sure that the comfort level of the kids remains high in this transition. This is a primary concern. And the clinical specialist can help a great deal in that regard. Each home is different. Each child is different. And Chris, as the clinical specialist, has to use her expertise to make sure the transition is a happy one, especially for the kids but also for the new Family-Teachers.

Chris will need to meet very, very frequently with the new couple each week in order to observe them as they live with and care for their new Boys Town family. It is important that the specialist visit the home at various times during the day. One day she may come during breakfast time and watch the Family-Teachers as they teach two boys to prepare breakfast and help them all get off to school. It is an opportunity to observe morning chores as well. On another visit, Chris will be there as soon as school is out and make special note of how each of the youth has a chance to go over his school day with a

Family-Teacher and review progress. On another visit, the specialist may stay for dinner and look at relationship development in the home. She may stay and observe a family conference after supper.

After each visit, Chris offers a great deal of praise and encouragement for the work the new Family-Teachers are doing and the family strengths they are building. Sincere praise and support are part and parcel of on-the-job training, in addition to making sure that each treatment plan is adapted as needs present themselves.

The Family-Teachers see the progress they are making. Chris emphasizes the skills and abilities that are developing. She sets specific skill goals for the Family-Teachers and follows up on their progress on subsequent visits.

Then on Friday morning, the clinical specialist and the Family-Teachers meet and go over each treatment plan. This helps the Family-Teachers brainstorm rationales for key skills individualized to each youth's interests, stage of development, and treatment goals. Chris indicates that the consistent use of rationales will help each youth understand the natural results of his behavior and the likely benefits of learning new ways of dealing with problems.

The clinical specialist makes a substantial investment in carefully helping the new Family-

Teachers develop skills and in teaching them to implement the philosophy of family life.

No matter how long Family-Teachers or Assistants have been working with our youth, there are always, always cases that stump even the best and most experienced of our veteran Family-Teachers. The clinical specialist is there to help provide answers. And like all professionals, if Chris doesn't know the answers, she knows where to get them. It's a real team effort.

In addition, veteran couples need to learn the latest techniques just as new couples do. Advances are being made every day in the behavioral sciences. All of us here at Boys Town need to be kept abreast. If we work as a team we will all learn more and help kids better.

The clinical specialist is also available for crisis intervention. There are times when a youth acts out and fails to respond to a Family-Teacher's best efforts. Intervention by the clinical specialist not only provides a fresh face and fresh ideas, but also gives the Family-Teachers the ability to work with their other six or seven kids and not neglect them. It really is a team effort.

Whenever there is a hint of a suicide ideation, the clinical specialist is summoned immediately to the home to do an evaluation based on the Suicide Prevention Scale. "An ounce of prevention…"

A teacher who presents the same material in the same way year after year without adding anything new soon becomes bored and then burns out. So, too, can Family-Teachers and all staff who work with kids. The clinical specialist's job is to make sure there is a high level of interest, excitement, and joy in the process of learning new ways to help kids get better.

One of the reasons for Boys Town's success is our clinical consultation system. Far too many child-care agencies provide a brief preservice learning opportunity and then staff immediately go on the line and there is very little, if any, clinical consultation. We believe that the clinical consultation services need to be as numerous and as intense as possible.

One of the problems many agencies face in dealing with wards of the state is that state agencies usually do not provide funding for ongoing training or clinical consultation services. And that means they are neglected. I would not want a physician who had learned nothing new since his graduation from medical school ten years ago to be treating our children. Neither should we allow youth-care workers to be without ongoing training. It's that important.

In summary, the clinical specialist and clinical director are important guiding members of the treatment team. Through direct observations, treatment planning visits, data reviews, crisis intervention, telephone consultation, and friendship building, Family-Teachers can develop some professional skills and receive the encouragement, information, and advice that they need.

Chapter 6

Evaluation

*E*valuation is the third of the four key elements of the Family Home Program. Evaluation simply means accountability to insure quality care and the highest level of treatment success possible. It is a performance assurance and performance improvement system.

Let's start with an example. Each year for the past four years, Louise and Mike Andrews have been certified by Boys Town as professional Family-Teachers. Meeting Boys Town's rigorous certification criteria means that Mike and Louise have consistently provided a safe, loving family environment. It means that their kids like and respect them. Each child is getting better, learning important skills, developing relationships, and more and more taking charge of his or her own treatment and life through self-discipline. It means that their kids are happy here at Boys Town. It means that their own religious practices have been inculcated. To be certified, Mike and Louise also have to work successfully and cooperatively with parents, teachers, and social service professionals.

How can Boys Town be sure that children are safe, secure, and happy and that they are receiving good treatment and getting better? How can Boys Town know the services provided by Mike and Louise are as good as we claim they are? How can judges and probation officers know this? How can anyone who really cares about these children know this? Boys Town's extensive evaluation systems provide the information necessary to assess the quality of home life and services provided by all Boys Town staff in all Boys Town sites each year.

Evaluation systems help provide a safe environment for the kids. They help assure the overall quality of care and treatment. They are designed to help Family-Teachers as they work with each child. In addition, evaluation results accumulated across the many couples who live and work at Boys Town also help the Internal Audit Division assure the quality of the overall organization. Evaluation systems help keep everything focused on the kids and what is best for them.

Ask the Kids: The Youth Evaluation

One way to know whether or not kids are safe, secure, and happy is to ask them. Larry has lived with the Andrews for six months. Before coming to live with Mike and Louise he had been placed in foster homes and detention centers. He was involved in joy riding, running away, and was frequently suspended from school. Before he came to Boys Town a lot of people had been asked to evaluate Larry and his progress. No one had ever asked Larry what he thought, at least not until he came to live at Boys Town.

In a private interview, a professional evaluator asks each youngster in the Family Home his or her opinions about the effectiveness, fairness, pleasantness, and concern of the Family-Teachers, the pleasantness of the other kids in the home, and the progress the child feels he or she is making toward solving important problems in life.

After each child is interviewed, all the information is pooled and edited to protect the anonymity of each child. For Mike and Louise, this means they will know the opinions of all their young men, including Larry. However, they will not be able to tell which comments and ratings were provided by which child. The Andrews have found the comments by their children both heartwarming and thought-provoking. The children's opinions are taken seriously and are used as a major source of information to make the decision about Mike and Louise's certification.

During the same interview "staff practice" questions are asked. The evaluator will ask Larry and every other child about potentially abusive practices that any staff member may have engaged in with them or with any other kids in the home or about any possible abuse (physical, emotional, or sexual) of one youth by another youth. Answers to these questions are critical. Our kids understand that Boys Town must be a safe place. When a child's well-being is at stake, we need to act promptly. The youth understand that anonymity is promised in all questions unless "there is threat of harm to self or others."

By now you are surely curious to see the list of some of the actual questions asked of our kids in our "youth evaluation." Here they are:

Youth Consumer Questions

1. Think about the reasons you were placed in the program. How satisfied are you that your Family-Teachers have been able to help you work on those areas?

2. How satisfied are you that your Family-Teachers have made it clear to you what your targeted areas are?

3. How satisfied are you that your Family-Teachers are teaching skills that will help you when you leave Boys Town? (independent living skills, social skills)

4. How satisfied are you that your Family-Teachers care enough about you to help you? For example, spend time with you or help you if you have problems.

5. How satisfied are you with the chances you have to help make decisions in your home? (vote at Family Meeting, listen to your opinions, review consequences)

6. Overall, how satisfied are you that your Family-Teachers are fair? (give what is deserved, no favoritism)

7. Overall, how satisfied are you with the pleasantness of your Family-Teachers? (friendly, smiling, joking, fun, enjoyable)

8. How satisfied are you that your Family-Teachers are trying to help you get along better with others? (other youth in the home, friends, classmates, parents, teachers, employers)

9. How satisfied are you that your Family-Teachers are actively supporting your religious education? (prayer at meal time, attendance at church, religious holidays)

10. Overall, how satisfied are you with your level of happiness with your Family-Teachers?

11. How satisfied are you that your Family-Teachers motivate you to try your best to learn the skills being taught in this home?

12. How many times per week does Family Meeting occur?

Staff Practice Questions

1. Has any staff or youth at Boys Town said or done anything to cause you to give high or low ratings on the Youth Consumer? If yes, has this caused you to change your ratings on the questions you just answered?

2. Has any staff member who works at Boys Town ever hurt you in any way, for example, kicked, slapped, grabbed, or swore at you?

3. Has any staff member who works at Boys Town ever forced you to do something that you did not want to do, such as something illegal or sexual?

4. Has any staff member who works at Boys Town made inappropriate remarks or harassed you in any way?

5. Has any staff member who works at Boys Town threatened you in any way?

6. Has any staff member who works at Boys Town asked you not to report information about themselves or others?

7. If you wanted to talk to your Clinical/Site Director, Residential Clinical Specialist or Father Peter, has any staff member who works at Boys Town stopped you or told you no?

These next questions deal with the
other youth in your home or on campus.

8. Is any other youth hurting you or threatening
   to hurt you? (intimidate you, hit, kick, slap, or
   bully you)

9. Has any other youth on campus forced you to
   do something illegal or sexual that you did not
   want to do?

10. Has any youth made inappropriate remarks or
    harassed you in any way?

If a youth describes an event that clearly does
not substantiate the response, the youth is
thanked and asked if there are any other
instances. Brief notes may even be made to
avoid differential reinforcement.

If there is any hint whatsoever of impropriety
by an adult with regard to our youth, Child
Protective Services are notified immediately of
the allegations and our Internal Audit Division
immediately begins an investigation. If the
allegations are serious, Boys Town's legal
counsel notifies the County Attorney and other
law enforcement agencies as necessary.

Striking a youngster even once results in
immediate termination of the adult. Our kids
have experienced enough violence already in
their lives. It just won't help them.

The reason why such violence occurs only rarely is that any organization that has sensitive indicators of possible abuse finds such measures to be preventive as well as remedial. For example, at Boys Town it is usually the Family-Teacher who will alert the clinical specialist about a possible violation of a youth's rights. This self-reporting is a key component to creating a safe place.

A judgment must be made in each case depending on the severity of the incident. The consequence for the staff person may range from termination to an official reprimand or increased monitoring for a period of time to complete exoneration. If the evidence indicates that no abuse occurred, the situation is sometimes difficult because reputations are often affected by the investigation process. In these cases, the investigators go back to each person (adult or child) who had been interviewed to explain the total facts of the case and to caution them against spreading rumors or discussing the case with others.

But Boys Town does not stop there. After any incident the program managers meet to discuss how the situation could have been prevented. Where did things go wrong? Was the wrong person selected and hired? Does the training program need to be changed? Was the clinical specialist doing enough monitoring and training?

Does the treatment program need to be modified? Or were the circumstances so unique that they are not likely to happen again? This helps to improve the program as changes are made and helps to keep attention focused on providing a safe environment for each youngster at Boys Town.

In addition to these conscientious efforts at detection and remediation, a great deal is done to prevent problems and to promote a safe, secure environment. At Boys Town, there are several feedback systems and evaluation systems geared to high standards for care and low tolerances for abuse or potentially harmful practices. Many problems are prevented simply by implementing very high standards for care and having the systems in place to monitor the processes and outcomes for kids.

The Family Home Program itself is the basic element in promoting a safe, helpful environment and in preventing abuse. The treatment program guides staff interactions with kids. That guidance is effective because of the efforts to recruit and select the best Family-Teachers and to train them to use treatment procedures humanely and sensitively. Support, help, and continued training through consultation provide further assistance.

In addition to these formal systems, an open, natural home environment is encouraged through frequent guest visits to each Family Home. Clinical specialists, clinical directors, administrators, parents, relatives, and community visitors are often in the home. Casual observations during these visits can provide further information about the health, happiness, and well-being of each child. Do the kids seem happy? Are the children comfortable around the Family-Teachers? Do the kids appear healthy and well-clothed? Do the kids speak positively and sincerely about their Family-Teachers and their Boys Town family? Is the home in good repair? Of course, considerable judgment by a thoroughly trained observer is sometimes required to see the signs of potential abuse or to conclude that abuse is occurring in a home. Nevertheless it is better to be overly sensitive and to investigate even the slightest hint of abuse. The safety of the children must come first. They have suffered enough already.

We put employees through a rigorous screening process including a thorough criminal background check. We have a state-of-the-art prevention process and early warning system. Yet, despite our screening process and all of these systems, it is impossible to read a person's innermost thoughts. And so we rigorously investigate any allegations or hints of impropriety. We turn them over to the County Attorney's office in accord with the dictates of the law.

Father Flanagan did not tolerate abuse or harm to children and neither do we. That a child might be hurt by his or her caretakers is an outrage. It cries to heaven. We live in a society where kids are routinely thrown away. That is even more reason why we need to stand firm and have a higher standard than even the law requires.

Ask Others: The Consumer Evaluation

Asking others who are concerned about each child can also help determine the quality of services. Larry's mother, his teachers and principal, his probation officer, and the judge who recommended his placement at Boys Town will all be asked to rate and comment on the services provided by the Andrews. Have the Andrews communicated frequently enough with you? Are Mike and Louise cooperative? Does Larry seem happy and well adjusted when he comes to school or visits at home? Does Larry seem to handle problems better? Like the youth evaluation, the ratings and opinions on these "consumer evaluations" are summarized and reported back to the couple and their community administrators. This consumer information also will help indicate whether or not the Andrews will be certified.

Here is the list of actual questions asked of parents/guardians and judges/social agency personnel:

Consumer Evaluation for Parents

1. How satisfied are you with the amount of cooperation and assistance you have received from the Family-Teachers who are working with your child?

2. How satisfied are you that you can talk freely with the Family-Teachers and call them about any problem you may have with your child?

3. How satisfied are you with the pleasantness of the Family-Teachers when you talk with them or when they write to you?

4. How satisfied are you that the Family-Teachers have helped your child?

5. Any comments, opinions, or suggestions about the Family-Teachers or Boys Town would be appreciated.

Consumer Evaluation for Judges and Agency Personnel

1. How satisfied are you that the Family-Teachers are doing an effective job in correcting the problems of this youth who has been placed in their care?

2. How satisfied are you with the amount of cooperation you have received from the Family-Teachers in their interactions with your agency concerning this youth?

3. How satisfied are you with the level of communication you have had with the Family-Teachers concerning this youth?

4. How satisfied are you with the pleasantness of interactions you have had with the Family-Teachers?

5. Any comments, suggestions, or additional information concerning the Family-Teachers or their home would be appreciated.

The opinions expressed by the kids, their parents/guardians, and other people who have a stake in the program are very important. Doing a good job with the kids depends upon the cooperation and help these other people are willing to provide. The Family-Teachers can help the youth progress at a faster pace if the youngsters see their Family-Teachers as being fair and concerned about them. The probation officers can provide more effective help and encouragement to a youngster if the Family-Teachers are cooperative and pleasant. The parents are often willing to try new things with their child if the Family-Teachers are helpful in solving problems. Thus the consumer evaluation serves not only as an early warning signal for problems, it also is an important indicator of the helpfulness of the treatment environment in a Boys Town Family Home.

Accuracy of Information

Can the opinions of the kids and the other consumers be trusted? How do you know that the kids didn't get together ahead of time and decide to "get their Family-Teachers" by giving them low scores on the evaluation? How do you know that the Family-Teachers didn't threaten the kids or promise some big reward to get the kids to give them high scores on the evaluation? How do you know that the school teacher knows what he is talking about when he describes an incident where a youngster had missed a meal as a consequence for something he or she had done wrong?

The simple answer to all these questions is that if you ask enough questions and get enough information from a sufficient number of sources, consistent themes begin to appear. Thus, the same information may mean different things as more facts are brought together. For example, low scores from most of the youth initially might be interpreted as reflecting low levels of teaching by the Family-Teachers. If further investigation brings to light some collusion among the kids, then the low scores might be interpreted as reflecting a very poor relationship between the Family-Teachers and the youngsters. In either case, low scores are meaningful and bring attention to some problem in the home.

How do you know what high scores mean from the kids? Do they reflect what they really think? Several things are done to help ensure that the scores and comments really reflect the kids' opinions. First, highly skilled evaluators interview each child privately to avoid peer pressure. Second, the evaluators have been taught to use interview skills that help to get at the true facts, positive or negative. Finally, during the interview the evaluator specifically asks each youngster whether he or she feels the Family-Teachers have attached any special conditions to the outcome of the evaluation. In other words, the evaluator must be convinced that the high scores are a true reflection of the kids' opinions and feelings.

How about the teacher in school who reports that a youngster was deprived of a meal? Any time such a report is made, an investigation is launched by interviewing the adult to get more specifics about the incident and then by interviewing the youngster, Family-Teachers, and others who may have been involved. Sometimes a youngster will feel comfortable talking to a teacher or social worker and tell that person about his concerns. Even though it may be only one complaint to one teacher by one child, such allegations are treated seriously.

All such allegations are thoroughly investigated because if the incident happened, such practices must be stopped immediately and the situation rectified. The kids must feel that they can trust the adults to protect them and help them. If the incident did not happen, the teacher and others need to know the true facts so the reputations of the Family-Teachers and of the home are not damaged.

Also, false allegations say something about the youngster and his or her treatment needs. If a youngster is unhappy with his Family-Teachers to the point of making false accusations, this is important information that can lead to changes in the treatment approach to enhance relationship development or to change goals to teach honest or appropriate ways for a boy to raise concerns.

A Look at the Home

The skills of the Family-Teachers as they interact with the kids are assessed by a professional evaluator who visits the Family Home. The evaluator is an expert in the Boys Town Family Home Program and has been specially trained as an observer and evaluator. When the evaluator visited the Andrews' Family Home, Larry got to take her on a tour of the home and help explain the way the family makes decisions by talking over issues and voting. Larry and the other kids in the home mostly followed their daily routine while the evaluator was there.

The evaluator was pleasant and friendly and was treated like other visitors to their home.

In addition to the tour of the home, the evaluator talks with the youngsters and observes the interaction patterns as they occur between the Family-Teachers and youth and among the youngsters. During the course of the visit, the evaluator assesses the teaching skills of the Family-Teachers, the self-government system that is operating in the home, the relationships among adults and youngsters, the actual skills of the youth, the quality of family-style living, the proper use of the Boys Town Family Home Program, and the physical condition of the home. By observing directly how the Family-Teachers work with the kids and by visiting the home and getting a feel for the atmosphere of the home, the evaluator can make a fair assessment of the skills of the Family-Teachers.

Program Evaluation Information

The youth evaluation, consumer evaluation, and in-home visit by the evaluator each provide important and useful information about the safety and helpfulness of the treatment environment. As important as this information is, it is available only periodically. This is why Boys Town created a program evaluation system that provides a steady flow of information about the activities in each Family Home.

Each month, Mike and Louise Andrews receive a report containing program evaluation information about their home. They and their clinical specialist review information in more than eighty areas such as number of runaways, number of admissions, number of youth problems at admission, school grades and attendance, school suspensions, number of positive or negative departures, length of stay, and so on. By looking at the information on individual kids they can see that Larry has not run away for the past six months and has run away only twice since he came to Boys Town – not bad for a kid who ran away seven times the year before that. The Andrews and their clinical specialist also can see that the eight boys in the Andrews' home averaged very few absences from school per quarter – a very good record for kids who had great difficulties attending school prior to Boys Town. This information helps to fill in the gaps between the other periodic evaluations and helps to promote a constant focus on the quality of care for children.

Family-Teacher Certification

The decision to certify a couple as professional Family-Teachers is based on a convergence of information from all four parts of the evaluation system. Criteria must be met on 1) the youth evaluation ("ask the kids"), 2) the consumer evaluation ("ask others"), 3) the in-home visit by the evaluator ("a look at the home"), and 4) the program evaluation information must be generally trending in the right direction.

All the evaluation information is reviewed by the Boys Town Evaluation Review Committee composed of knowledgeable child-care administrators as well as the couple's clinical director. The Evaluation Review Committee looks at the multiple sources of information and looks for convergent themes or issues. The committee then determines whether or not to certify a couple. If the decision is not to certify the couple, the conditions and time frame for the couple to try again are specified. This is usually thirty days later. If the couple fails this second evaluation as well, they are terminated.

The evaluation and certification process also helps some couples make the decision that Family-Teaching may not be for them. They have tried hard but still fall short of Boys Town's standards for care in spite of their hard work and the help of their clinical specialist.

The accountability prompted by this certification process is crucial to the quality of care each youth receives. It is also crucial to the quality of the support services received by Family-Teachers. The certification process serves as the "conscience" of the Boys Town Family Home Program. Not only does it encourage

consistent high quality program implementation
by Family-Teachers, but it also helps improve
Family-Teacher selection, training, and consultation processes. The extensive data indicate in
what areas couples are excelling and in what
areas they need more assistance to provide the
best possible care.

The certification process occurs annually for
each couple. The process credits those Family-
Teachers who meet or exceed expectations and
also serves as the first step in a career ladder for
Family-Teachers. Salary increments, opportunities
for advanced training, and opportunities to move
into administrative positions are all based on the
quality of services provided by Family-Teachers.
The excellent, consistent care provided by
Family-Teachers is reflected in their certification.

Internal Program Audit

The Internal Program Audit Division is one of
the most important ways to insure the safety of
our youth as well as quality of our programs.

This function is so important that the Internal
Program Auditor reports directly to the National
Board of Trustees. A committee of the National
Board reviews with the Internal Program Auditor
all the factors so that our Trustees can be assured
that we are living up to the standards that we
hold for ourselves as well as the standards of
accrediting organizations.

In addition, in each of our Boys Town sites, there is an Advisory Board which looks at quality assurance and quality improvement under the title of Performance Assurance and Performance Improvement. This is a vital function so important for the integrity of our programs and the assurance that our children are safe, happy, and getting better.

Chapter 7

Administration

*A*dministration is the fourth key element in the Boys Town Family Home Program. Family-Teachers have wide-ranging responsibilities for meeting the needs of children. With so much responsibility and authority vested in the married couple living with the youth, each Family Home requires sensitive and supportive administration. Boys Town has designed its administrative functions to meet the needs of Family-Teachers – not vice versa. Since the welfare of the individual child is the most critical concern, the organization must serve the staff who are assigned the most critical child-care roles. Administrative procedures must be there to ease the burden of Family-Teachers and facilitate the accomplishment of treatment goals for each youth and his or her family. In addition, Family-Teachers must be paid a generous wage. They are professionals and need to be paid as professionals. The same is true of Assistant Family-Teachers.

This kind of support is appreciated by Mary Helen and Dennis Murphy. On Wednesday evening they sat down with a couple of their boys to review next week's menu and to go through the newspaper to look for grocery sales and coupons. As they made their grocery list they decided to buy meat at one store, milk and cheese at the dairy, and the rest of their food at another supermarket. The next night after the Family Meeting, Dennis put the home's checkbook in his pocket and took the two boys out to do the shopping. The boys learned a lot about shopping for the best buy, planning meals, staying within a budget, unit pricing, avoiding impulse buying, and even how to be polite to other shoppers.

The decision to promote flexibility and convenience through a home checking account was not just an administrative decision. It was also a treatment decision. In fact, nearly every administrative decision impacts treatment. For example, if there are time-consuming, cumbersome procedures for obtaining funds for family outings in the community, Family-Teachers are less likely to arrange family outings on a regular basis. In turn this means that kids would then have fewer opportunities to learn community living skills and to practice new skills in relevant settings. Similarly, if pre-set consequences for rule violations are established by administrators, then Family-Teachers lose the opportunity to individualize treatment and to have their "family" participate in rational problem-solving sessions that strengthen each child's ability to think, reason, and exercise good judgment.

A second aspect of administrative support involves providing adequate resources so that Family-Teachers can devote their skill and energy toward helping each child. Administrators provide family-style homes with adequate private space for Family-Teachers and their natural children. They also see to it that the home is suitably furnished, supplied, and in good repair. Survey results indicate that adequate living space is correlated with increased Family-Teacher tenure. Of course, Family-Teacher tenure affects the amount of time each child spends in treatment with experienced, qualified professionals.

In addition to providing physical and financial resources, administrative support systems include arranging for staffing and supervision systems. In terms of staffing, each couple employs an Assistant who works at least forty hours per week for them. This Assistant is similarly trained and functions as a full member of the team under the direction of the Family-Teachers.

In terms of supervision, each couple is assigned a clinical specialist and an administrative specialist. The clinical specialist provides treatment support. The administrative specialist provides support in the whole area of budgets, home furnishings, repairs, and anything that has to do with the physical plant.

Professional Family-Teachers who are prepared well for their treatment tasks and who feel the support, encouragement, and assistance of their clinical specialist, administrative specialist, and administrators are less likely to be frustrated by the kids, feel alone in their jobs, or develop the "what's the use" attitude typical of emotionally exhausted staff. It is up to administration to make sure that all the technical systems are coordinated and focused on helping the youngsters and the Family-Teachers.

Administration also goes beyond these direct support services for Family-Teachers. Policies and procedures for overall program operations must be established. Criteria for youth admissions, referral sources, and cost-reimbursement contracts must be established or negotiated. Family-Teachers, Assistant Family-Teachers, trainers, clinical specialists, administrative specialists, evaluators, clinical directors, and administrators must be recruited and hired. Licenses must be obtained and regulations met. Procedure manuals must be thought through, written, and kept up to date. Budgets need to be established and monitored and funding secured. All service and administrative functions must be integrated and coordinated. Evaluation data must be reviewed and interpreted. National trends need to be anticipated, and plans for the future need to be made. The list goes on. It takes a lot of work to make a human service program function smoothly to benefit the kids.

Because of the importance of administrators to the overall functioning of the organization, they too are evaluated regularly. Twice each year the Family-Teachers, teachers, and other direct-care staff evaluate their administrators by answering such questions as: Do you feel free to discuss your feelings about your job? Are you asked for your ideas and opinions? Is your advice used? Are your decisions supported? Does your supervisor know the solutions to most of the problems you encounter? Do you have the resources to do your job? Is your supervisor pleasant? Is evaluation information used punitively? The ratings and comments provided by Family-Teachers, teachers, and others help to bring attention to areas of strength and areas that need more effort. It helps keep the whole organization focused on the primary caregivers and the support they feel for getting the job done with the kids.

Administration must provide enlightened leadership so that everything done at Boys Town has the care and treatment of kids as its primary goal. The Associate Executive Director for the Home Campus is responsible for all of our four systems being effective and operative: training, clinical consultation, evaluation, and administration. The Associate Executive Director for Boys Town USA provides the same for all Boys Town sites outside of the Home Campus. Establishing a sense of shared mission, cooperation, and mutuality of interest helps promote the kind of hard work and dedication required to improve the quality of care each child receives.

As you can see, administration at Boys Town is proactive and planned rather than just reactive. Instead of just going from one crisis to another, a more thoughtful approach is taken. What problems seem to be repetitious? What can be changed to prevent such problems in the future? Which goals are not being accomplished fully? How can training, consultation, evaluation, and administrative systems be changed to promote greater progress toward those goals? Over time, administrators continue to look at evaluation data to help find problems and to help make administrative procedures more systematic, thorough, and sensitive to the needs of the youngsters and Family-Teachers.

Chapter 8

Religion in Family Life

This chapter is a brief introduction to the central place that religion plays in helping children and families find healing and hope through Boys Town.

Most programs for children and families across America pay only lip service to the healing power of religion in a child or family's life. We know from experience that without solid spiritual underpinnings, our children will be swept out with the sea of despair, alienation, and bitterness.

Our founder, Father Flanagan, in his own day changed the way America thought of her abandoned and orphaned children. His convictions about the importance of religious formation for young people are summed up in his famous phrase: "Every boy (or girl) must learn to pray. How he (or she) prays is up to him (or her)."

What Father Flanagan meant is that there are two extremes which need to be avoided in Boys Town's programs if children are to get better. The first extreme is proselytism and the other is neglect of religion. Let's examine both.

Proselytism

Let's start with proselytism. Can you imagine what a stir Father Flanagan created way back in 1917 when he insisted on personally taking two of his first five boys who were Baptist to Baptist Sunday school every week without fail? In his day, if you went to a Catholic home for children, it didn't matter what you went in as, you all came out as Roman Catholics. And if you went to a Southern Baptist home for children, it didn't matter what you went in as, you all came out as Southern Baptists. And if you went to a Methodist home for children, it didn't matter what you went in as, you all came out as Methodists.

Father Flanagan's view prevails today at Boys Town. So if a youth comes from a Methodist background, we're going to try to make him a better Methodist. If he comes from a Lutheran background, we're going to try to make him a better Lutheran. And if he is a Jew, we're going to try to make him a better Jew and insist that he go weekly to the synagogue. And if he is a follower of Islam, by golly he's going to the Islamic Center every week.

In other words, we do not proselytize. It is important to understand why. It is not because we are indifferent. It is not because we think "one religion is as good as another." It is because the children who come to us are a "captive population." They are prisoners of tragic circumstances. Yes, they are prisoners as much as those behind bars. The difference is that the bars for them are bars of abandonment, abuse, neglect, violence, and suicide. There are special ethical rules for captive populations. One of them is that you should not proselytize. We have too much power, and they have too little freedom. For this reason, proselytism would violate the covenant of loyalty that we have with them. We stand before the Lord ourselves and make an account of our stewardship.

Neglect of Religion

"Every boy (or girl) must learn to pray." Today in America this is not considered politically correct. But it is true and it is necessary because kids can't get better without it. Let's go into some detail.

How many homes for children do I know, especially those run by the state, where on Sunday there is a nondescript, uninspiring optional worship opportunity? The state gives only lip service to religious needs. There are no prayers at meals. Kids are not encouraged to pray at bedtime. They are not encouraged to read their Scriptures. And they are simply not taught that if you are powerless before the forces in your life, that you desperately need to get in touch with a "Higher Power."

It is silly and naive to believe that we can build a moral society without belief in a Creator whose moral laws are to govern our lives. Basing moral norms on the majority opinion of a society is perilous indeed. It does not imbue children with private virtue, and without such virtue they cannot get better. A boy or girl who lies, cheats, steals, and acts out sexually will not get better. Father Flanagan was right: "Every boy (or girl) must learn to pray."

Let me tell two stories that illustrate the importance of religion in the lives of our children.

Amy was 14 years old when she came to the Village of Boys Town. Her presenting problems were drugs, alcohol, sexual acting out, stealing, and truancy from school. We did not know until after she arrived that she had been repeatedly sexually abused by her father from the third grade on until she reported it six months after her arrival on our doorstep.

Then there is Jesse. He is 15 years old. His family moves a lot. He was in three psychiatric hospitals before arriving at Boys Town having attempted to take his life five times. His father is a raging alcoholic who has beaten Jesse in his rages ever since the boy was 3 years old.

Amy and Jesse have four characteristics in common:

1. Powerlessness. Amy feels powerless to stop the abuse that has been happening to her. Month after month, year after year she was powerless before the advances of her father. In her mind, her father was all-powerful.

The first characteristic of Jesse is also a terrible, oppressive feeling of powerlessness because of the beatings his father, year after year, gave him. There was nothing he could do to stop it. In Jesse's eyes, his father was all-powerful.

Both Jesse and Amy describe their fathers as having all the power. What is "all-powerful" a description of? A description of God. Yes, Amy's father and Jesse's father displaced God from these children's lives and made it impossible for them to get in touch with a Higher Power. No wonder they had lost hope. For the all-powerful person in their lives was malevolent.

2. My Fault. The second characteristic of both Amy and Jesse is they blame themselves. Jesse says it is "my fault that my father beats me." Why does he say that? Remember back when he was 3 years old when his father first beat him? He ran to his mother who said: "If you wouldn't make so much noise, your father wouldn't beat you." That was repeated over and over, year after year. Whose fault was it? Jesse's. His father said so often: "If you weren't such a disobedient and disrespectful kid, you wouldn't need this discipline."

How can Amy possibly think it is her fault? It's easy to explain. Amy will tell you that she always liked some of the attention her father gave her. She didn't like the sexual part. But at first she liked being called "daddy's special girl" who had "special privileges" and got "special things." Her father told her repeatedly: "I know you like it." And again: "If you hadn't started jumping on my lap with your little nightgown on when you were in the third grade, this would have never happened."

Jesse's father says it's not his fault. "You'd drink too if you had all the troubles I had." And Amy's father says it's not his fault: "Isn't it better she learns this from me than some hippie?"

So both Amy and Jesse say it is their fault, and they feel powerless to stop it – even more reason to have no hope.

3. **A Secret.** The third characteristic of Jesse and Amy is what has happened to them is a secret. Amy's father told her: "If you ever tell your mother, first she won't believe it, or if she does

believe it, you'll be thrown out of the house." Well, she told her mother, and her mother didn't believe her at first. But when her mother believed her, guess who got sent out of the house? Her father? No. Amy did. The victim has been punished.

How did Amy keep "the secret?" By getting into drugs, alcohol, stealing, and truancy. She was just known as "a wild kid." Who would have suspected how it all started?

How did Jesse keep "his secret?" By prosocial behavior. By doing well in school. He always had good grades. By playing in the band. He was well liked. In that way, nobody would possibly suspect that he was being such a bad person as to cause his father to beat him. The only thing he would not do is play sports. Why? Because to play sports you have to take your clothes off in the locker room, and people would see the black and blue marks. The problem with Jesse, of course, was that he could only stand it so long, and then he would try to put an end to his life. And when he did, people would say: "How could such a successful young man do that?"

4. **Love.** The fourth characteristic Amy and Jesse share may seem like a strange one. Amy loves her father and in some strange way, her father loves her. She just wishes he would act like a father. And Jesse loves his father. He just

wishes the beatings would cease and that his father would start going to A.A. And in some strange way, his father does love him.

Stop and think about it. Unless Jesse or Amy gets in touch with a Higher Power, they will forever feel powerless, without hope, and filled with guilt.

Religion isn't a luxury for Amy and Jesse. It's not a social nicety. It's an absolute necessity in their lives. Anyone familiar with A.A. understands its first principle: "I am powerless. I need to get in touch with the Higher Power."

We have far too many kids who look like Jesse and Amy. Far, far too many.

When children come to us they suffer from abandonment, neglect, physical, psychological, and sexual abuse as well as just about every kind of trouble a child has ever been afflicted with. All the technologies that we have described in the previous chapters – important as they are – will only initially help change the exterior behavior of our boys and girls.

After a few months in one of Boys Town's many programs, our boys and girls will begin to behave better on the surface. They will look like they have really made immense progress. But so far, up to that point, we have only touched the outside, the surface of things. It is only when the boy or girl allows the Lord into the heart and experiences a miracle of inner healing that the child then experiences release in his or her life of the goodness, the beauty, the faith, the hope, and love that are God's gracious gifts. It is only then that they make up their minds to use the skills we have taught them after they leave our program. Without getting in touch with God, the success of Boys Town's programs with all our immense technologies would count for nothing. That is why religion is a definite priority in all our programs for boys and girls who come to us. And that is why we respect and enhance the religious traditions of youth who come to us.

Goals for Religious Training

Family-Teachers, Assistant Family-Teachers, and all our staff have the awesome responsibility of inculcating sound religious practices while at the same time exercising caution lest they inhibit by proselytism the free exercise of conscience of our youth. We at Boys Town have set eight specific goals for the religious development of youth in Boys Town programs.

1. **The first goal is for each youth to appreciate and cherish his or her fundamental relationship with God who loves and understands him or her.**

   We who work with kids are images of God for them. Our primary obligation is to help our boys and girls realize that God loves and understands them.

So often in the past, our kids have had either negative experiences of religion or almost no religious experience at all. The difficulties that have plagued their homes – alcoholism, a stressful divorce, domestic violence, abuse of every kind, suicide, abandonment – all have made God seem far away and indifferent to them. They need to see positive warm images of God, and all of us are there to provide them. No wonder we have to pray so hard. No wonder we who work here have to be people of ever-deepening faith.

2. Our second goal for religion is for each youth to become a role model of faith for all other youth in their house.

Family-Teachers and Assistant Family-Teachers, for example, have to lead the way by being role models in this regard for their youth. Role models are respected, admired people who make the faith life attractive by encouraging others in gentle and joyful ways to witness to their faith. As a role model, it is important that the attitude of Family-Teachers and all of us be such that it encourages religious life in our homes and programs.

3. The third goal in religious development is that each youth will attend church each Sunday or Sabbath.

Our youth need to be taught how to pray. They especially need to be taught that going to church is not like going to a concert or to a movie. It is not a place to be entertained although it should be a joyful and positive experience. It is a place where we go to let the good Lord "form us in the faith." When we go, we acceptingly listen to God's written words to us which are the Scriptures, His love letters to each of us. We do not just listen. We attend with open hearts and open minds. We wonder why the Lord would love us so in the midst of all our sorrows, and then we see why when we watch the good Lord Himself turn sorrow into joy.

The fresh message of all Holy Writ is that the Lord is attracted to the dark places of our lives where He Himself wants to enter into our darkness and be for us light which the darkness cannot overcome. We need to make church services an experience that is positive, and there are definite skills all of us can learn to be successful at this.

Family-Teachers, Assistant Family-Teachers, and staff need to manifest church attendance behavior which will allow the youth to view it as a very important family activity. In addition, Family-Teachers, Assistant Family-Teachers, and staff need time away to worship privately outside Boys Town and let their church minister to their own special needs as well.

4. **The fourth goal for religion at Boys Town is for each youth to learn the rudiments of his or her faith and practice, whether Christian or Jewish or Islamic.**

We live in an age that is becoming religiously illiterate. Learning about a religious tradition is as important as learning reading, mathematics, and so many other secular pursuits. But learning about the Lord is not the same as following Him. Our kids need to be disciples, not just students of religion.

All Boys Town personnel need to take it as a special responsibility to help a boy's or girl's faith life grow without proselytism, that is, without directly trying to influence the youngster to accept their own personal denominational preference.

5. **The fifth goal of religious development is for each youngster to become a person who prays regularly and appreciates the religious significance of special events.**

Prayer should be part of our home life. Every day before meals every Boys Town family prays together asking God's blessing. Family-Teachers and Assistants are teachers of prayer by example, by direct instruction, and by praise and appreciation. The prayers before meals and before meetings as well as morning and night prayers should be part of our daily lives. In addition, we celebrate with our kids the rich variety of religious traditions that surround the great events of Thanksgiving, Christmas, Easter, Passover, Hanukkah, birthdays, Baptismal days, and other personal events.

6. The sixth goal for religious development is for each youth to develop sound, solid religious home habits.

Religious home habits help create an atmosphere of warmth, an atmosphere we would like to pervade our homes. These habits include times for reflection, for private prayer, for reading the Holy Scriptures and other devotional books as well.

7. The seventh goal is for our kids to have the opportunity to develop a positive relationship with pastors and chaplains.

This is an integral part of religion in family life at Boys Town.

8. The eighth and final goal for religious development is that it will be encouraged in the life of each child at Boys Town in a balanced way – that is without overexaggeration or underexaggeration.

It should be clear by what you have read so far that Family-Teachers, Assistant Family-

Teachers, and staff are asked to be sound religious leaders in our homes and other programs. They are asked to draw out and utilize what the youth have learned and put it into practice at home. They are asked to initiate good sound religious practices and if they are successful, they will need to project warm images of God and His relationship with each one of us. It is in this way that Family-Teachers, Assistants, and others clearly function as key persons for the religious development of children and youth.

The religious development of each youth should be balanced, that is, without overemphasis or underemphasis.

Examples of overemphasis are:
- Excessive use of religious terms in every conversation with youth,
- Using God as the exclusive rationale for all behaviors,
- Only allowing religious music in the home,
- Only allowing religious books in the home,
- Misuse of prayer,
- Sermonizing instead of discussing,
- Playing religious tapes at top volume to "create a proper atmosphere."

Examples of underemphasis are:

- Discouraging the use of religious talk/ conversation,
- Avoiding the use of God as a rationale for any behaviors,
- Not allowing or encouraging religious music in the home,
- Not praying before meals,
- Not taking an active part in campus religious projects,
- Not helping with religion class homework in a positive, approving fashion,
- Being negative and unenthusiastic about Sunday services.

Finally, Family-Teachers, Assistant Family-Teachers, and staff spend time teaching their children appropriate church behavior. When our kids ask us why we spend so much time doing this, we give the following rationales:

1. You can't get better if you don't get in touch with a Higher Power. That's why Boys Town is more than a secular institution. It is committed to helping children grow spiritually. Learning how to worship is a big step in getting better.

2. If youth know how to worship appropriately, they will be likely to participate better because they will not be so self-conscious or awkward.

3. Participation in the service provides an opportunity to praise God by using the skills our youth are developing.

4. This is also a way to participate with many adults who are good role models for us and who are there to worship because they have discovered how you grow from powerlessness to power by letting the Lord into your life.

Let us conclude with a prayer which is found in *The Boys Town Prayer Book* and which the kids tell me is their very favorite prayer. It is Jesse's and Amy's favorite prayer too.

Dear Lord,

I have been very hard on myself. I make demands on myself which are too harsh. I judge myself too severely. I have put myself down too often. That is how I grew up. That is how I was taught. Dear Lord, I am putting myself in Your presence. I am one with You, God, as well as with others. I am not going to hurt myself or others anymore. I am now experiencing being cared for and guided by You, God. Dear Lord, please heal my soul, mind, and body and that of all people now. I rest in Your peace and healing today and forever.

Amen.

Chapter 9

Admission Criteria and Profiles of Some of Our Children

*W*ho can get into Boys Town's homes? Our basic rule is two-fold: We only take children who want to be here, and we only take children who are best helped here. If a child can be helped more by staying home and receiving counseling locally, then let's do that. If it is in the child's best interest to be hospitalized or even placed for a time in a more restrictive environment than Boys Town, then let's do that. Our basic rule for admission is: do what is in the best interest of the boy or girl. The first step in admissions is for a boy or girl to write to Father Peter and explain why he or she wants to come to Boys Town. We can't help a child get better unless the child wants to get better.

Boys Town has an Admissions Committee which tries to do what is in the best interest of the boy or the girl. It makes decisions on which boys and girls would be best helped by the Boys Town Family Home Program. Sometimes decisions are easy to make because it is very clear that a child still has an intact family and his or her problems are not so serious as to require removal from the home community. But oftentimes decisions are much more difficult. Parents are often desperate when they come to us. Their son or daughter is totally out of control, and they are at their wits' end. In cases such as those our admissions criteria sometimes seem unfair to parents who are hurting so badly. Why can't we take their son when we have taken a child of another family whom they know? Is it because the other family "knew somebody" or had more power? More often than not those feelings are based on frustration and parental agony rather than on anything else.

But Boys Town is not perfect. Sometimes we do make mistakes. Every once in a while, we goof – we overlook a child who belongs here or take a boy or girl who does not belong here. "To err is human; to forgive is divine." But we ask those of you who read this book to be patient with us and realize that we are trying to serve children in the way that best benefits each child.

We believe in the family. We believe in community-based alternatives. We believe that good child care should occur on a continuum beginning with the family and progress to more restrictive means only when necessary. What are the general guidelines or criteria which our committee uses in making decisions about accepting children into the program? They are listed below. Even though each boy's or girl's situation is unique, these admissions guidelines have proven helpful to us when making such decisions.

1. Boys Town provides long-term residential care in a non-restrictive, family-style setting.

Only boys and girls who are expected to stay at least twelve months (and preferably much longer) are admitted. Boys Town is a long-term agency. Children who need only short-term residential care are best served elsewhere. Many adolescents stay four years or more at Boys Town. The average length of stay is over eighteen months. In order to assure that long-term care is the least restrictive alternative for each child, Boys Town works with and through the social service agencies in the youth's own area, agencies which can best tell us whether or not the resources in the youth's community have been exhausted. All our boys and girls live with married couples in homes where family values such as love, honesty, affection, and responsibility are emphasized.

2. Boys Town works with youth whose behavioral or family problems are so serious that they need to be removed from their home community.

If the problems are not that serious, then Boys Town is not an appropriate placement for a child. Boys Town youth are functionally homeless. The boys and girls we admit are homeless either because their family no longer functions or because a public agency has taken custody of the children.

More than 70 percent of all Boys Town youth are known to have been abused in some way or another. Others, about 65 percent, have had formal court involvement for delinquent acts such as theft. Family counseling and family-based care should be attempted before a youth is considered for Boys Town. In fact, the typical youth has had three to four out-of-home placements such as foster homes or group homes before Boys Town. Well over 90 percent of the boys or girls who come to us are admitted through agencies such as juvenile courts or state social services. By working through these agencies, it can be determined that continued placement in the natural family or into foster families is not an option.

3. **Boys Town typically admits youth between 10 and 17 years old.**

   Since Boys Town provides long-term care, the typical child is admitted in this age range. However, the program serves children as young as 8 and as old as 19. For instance, an 8 or 9 year old might be admitted if an older sibling were coming to Boys Town. The average age of admission is 14.

   Ideally, all newly admitted youth will stay through high school graduation as both the residential and educational programs are oriented to long-term care. The most recent Boys Town High School graduating class of eighty-nine students had an average length of stay of more than three years.

4. **Boys Town provides a continuum of care to youth whose local support systems have broken down or are nonexistent.**

   The agencies which refer children to Boys Town are best equipped to know when local resources have been exhausted. Boys Town admits a wide spectrum of boys and girls suffering from abuse, abandonment, or serious neglect.

   A full 45 percent of youth were not attending any school immediately before coming – either because of expulsion from the public systems or habitual truancy. Local remedies were not successful.

Forty percent of the youth who come to Boys Town have been on probation or parole. Many youth have not been through the court system but became wards of state agencies after it was determined that their family was no longer an appropriate environment for them. These youth might be status offenders such as habitually truant, incorrigible, or neglected youngsters.

Boys Town provides a wide range of care for all of its youth. We offer not only basic care and treatment and family-style living for our youth, but special needs programs as well.

These include: the Residential Treatment Center at the Boys Town National Children's Hospital, specialized group homes for boys and girls, specialized treatment homes for younger children, and a respite house as well. For instance, there is the Intensive Teaching program for children already admitted to Boys Town but who have behavior problems which necessitate specialized care. There is the Transitional Living program for older youth who will not be returning to their families and need focused training in independent living skills. There is also a scholarship program and counseling services that provide support and direction after boys or girls leave Boys Town for further education or employment.

5. Boys Town admits youth into its homes whose needs can be met in an open, family-style, community-oriented environment.

Boys Town programs have a community-based philosophy. Youth are provided with age-appropriate responsibilities, freedoms, and opportunities. For example, youth live in a home much like any home. They may work at a local fast food restaurant, go shopping at the local mall, or ride their bike into the country with a friend.

While Boys Town cares for a wide range of youth such as adjudicated delinquents, status offenders, and abused/neglected children, there are some youth whose needs are not best met in an open environment such as a Boys Town Family Home. For example, while many Boys Town youth have suicidal attempts or ideation or substance abuse backgrounds, acutely suicidal or acutely drug dependent youth would not be good candidates for admission until after resolution of the suicide crisis and appropriate treatment or after successful completion of a chemical dependency program. This we encourage very much. Similarly, while many youth at Boys

Town have a history of serious aggressive behavior, youth who are actively dangerous to others would not be best served in a family-style environment. Perhaps these youth may be served by our RTC (Residential Treatment Center).

6. **Boys Town admits youth with serious academic difficulties, but who are functioning in the normal range of intelligence.**

   The typical Boys Town student is within the average range of intellectual functioning. However, the average Boys Town student is functioning about two to three years below grade level upon admission. Consequently, the grade school, high school, and vocational school provide special education services in small classes. Both due to the nature of the educational programs and the typical boy or girl in residence, Boys Town does not accept mildly or moderately retarded children. A full scale I.Q. of 80 or above is the normal guideline for intelligence. However it should be noted that more than one child has been labeled mildly or moderately retarded when in fact their difficulties are due to other factors. We have taken quite a few of these kind of children.

7. **As an aid in permanency planning, Boys Town admits youth whose parents or legal guardians agree to maintain their legal relationship.**

Permanency planning is central to Boys Town's program. Boys Town is not the legal guardian of any child served. A priority is given to children who no longer have a natural or adoptive parent. This is a longstanding tradition of the Home. Yet many, many youth are admitted whose natural or adoptive families still have legal guardianship. In all cases, Boys Town works with the referring agent and guardian to facilitate a successful permanency plan.

When youth have at least one natural or adoptive parent, Boys Town staff work both directly and through the referring agency to do everything in their power to facilitate family reunification. Often however, family problems are so serious and so long lasting as to frustrate our vast hopes here. But we keep trying. In situations where the referring agency has permanent guardianship, Boys Town works with them at facilitating the youth's transition in every case possible for a life with relatives or foster parents or directly – that happens so often – to independent living as a young adult. A long-term resource of scholarship opportunities for post-secondary education as well as aftercare crisis and vocational counseling provide long-term planning and life assistance to former residents.

8. Boys Town works with local and non-local youth.

About 40 percent to 50 percent of the children who come to the Village of Boys Town come from within a 200- to 300-mile radius of Omaha, Nebraska. However, Boys Town has residents from all of the fifty states and even a few youth from other countries. Because Boys Town is a national organization and receives support from the whole country, we feel it is important to give serious consideration to youth from every state who can best be served by Boys Town. In addition, Boys Town has services in eighteen states and the District of Columbia.

9. No child is denied admission for financial reasons.

Boys Town has always prided itself on taking children without regard for their ability to pay. Most boys and girls come from families which can pay little or nothing. They are most welcome. If public sources such as state social service agencies have money available to pay even a little something such as a small fraction of the cost of care, then Boys Town will solicit this cooperation.

Almost every family is asked to pay as little as $5.00 a month simply because it gives them a sense of participation and partnership in helping their boy or girl get better. If a child comes from a well-to-do family, then no one would expect them to be dispensed from contributing a greater amount to their son's or daughter's care. Only about 33 cents out of every program dollar spent on Boys Town youth come from direct payment by public agencies or private individuals.

About 66 cents out of every program dollar spent on our boys and girls come from the generosity of the American people in every state of the Union. Where exactly does this 66 cents come from? Father Flanagan began a Trust Fund in 1941, and it provides about 33 cents out of every program dollar each year for the care of children. In addition, the American people desiring to share in our Mission and work send us donations (direct gifts, wills, and bequests) to pay for about 33 cents. Every penny sent to us by the American people is spent in the care of our children in the year in which it is received. Not one penny of their donation is spent on administrative expenses or the cost of solicitation, both of which are paid for by Father Flanagan's Trust Fund.

10. Boys Town accepts some private placements but would much prefer the involvement of social service agencies in the youth's own community.

Sometimes people wonder why Boys Town prefers that its boys and girls are admitted through local agencies in the youth's home town. One reason is mentioned above: it is to assure that the child receives care in the least restrictive environment.

Another very important reason is simply this: boys and girls usually show remarkable progress within three to four months of their arrival at Boys Town. Parents are at that time often tempted to believe that their child is "fixed." They are tempted to withdraw the child, and thus Boys Town is no longer able to help precisely at that crucial juncture in the child's life when much progress can be made. There is nothing more detrimental to a child than to be pulled out of a treatment program too soon. Placement through hometown agencies helps parents resist this temptation. On the other hand, if parents move or "disappear" while a child is with us (as happens sometimes), it is easier for a local agency to discover their whereabouts or at least work with relatives.

The community-based philosophy of Boys Town considers public or private agencies in the local area as partners in helping provide the best possible continuum of care for a child, thus maximizing the possibility of reintegration of the family.

11. Persons interested in placing a boy or girl at Boys Town should contact:

The Admissions Office
Father Flanagan's Boys' Home
Boys Town, Nebraska 68010
1-800-989-0000

Profiles of Some of Our Kids

Abused, neglected, homeless – these are the children who seek shelter at Boys Town. But these terms cover a multitude of horrors.

The mind and spirit as well as the body can be battered. A child rejected, terrorized, or corrupted by parents or other adults is as homeless as any orphan.

Who are our children? As difficult as it may be to accept or understand, they are:

David (age 10)

David's young, unmarried mother apparently hated herself and took this hatred out on her son. David repeatedly heard his mother scream at him, "You're just no damn good to anybody. Why don't you do the world a favor and kill yourself?" At one time, she gave him sleeping pills, instructing him to take them all. David lived unsuccessfully with his grandmother for a year before coming to Boys Town.

Gina (age 16)

Gina's father thought teenage girls needed strict rules and tight supervision. For any infraction of his rules, Gina was grounded for days at a time, locked in her room, and not permitted to go to school. She had to ask her father for permission to eat, sleep, speak, even use the bathroom. If she complained, her father would chain her to a radiator in a closet and leave her there overnight. Gina finally escaped one day and never returned home.

Tom (age 14)

Tom's parents fought continually, and he (his grades, clothing, haircut, choice of music) was often the focus of their disagreements. In tears after these arguments, his mother would turn to Tom and shout, "It's your fault. If you'd leave, everything would be fine." At age 12, Tom ran away and lived on the streets. When he was picked up by the police and returned home, his parents told him they didn't want him. He lived in two different group homes before coming to Boys Town.

Janice (age 15)

Janice had been sexually abused by her father from the age of 6. She was terrified of meeting people and had no friends at school. Unable to concentrate for more than a few minutes, she had already flunked two grades. If she refused her father's sexual advances, he would take a gun and put it to his head, telling her that he would kill himself if she didn't submit. She lived with foster parents but ran away four times.

Brad (age 16)

Brad was often in trouble at school and with the police. At 14, he had a long police record, having been picked up for drunkenness, shoplifting, fighting, and truancy. Brad's father had encouraged the delinquency – buying him beer, approving of Brad's bragging about his exploits, and arguing with school and court authorities who tried to discipline Brad. His father was proud his son was "no sissy." Brad spent time in a lockup facility before coming to Boys Town.

Keith (age 12)

An alcohol and drug abuser, Keith's father turned violent during his frequent binges. Keith would be beaten until his father fell asleep, exhausted. Sometimes Keith came home to find the doors and windows locked, his father yelling threats at him, warning him not to try getting into the house. On those nights, Keith slept outside. Keith ran away from two group homes before coming to Boys Town.

Russell (age 11)

After her divorce, Russell's mother found that the men she met had little interest in her 9-year-old son. Soon she stopped bringing boyfriends into the home and often stayed out all night, occasionally disappearing for several days at a stretch. Russell began to lose weight, appeared at school in torn, dirty clothing, and was discovered trying to forge his mother's signature on school notes. His mother refused to meet with teachers about Russell's failing grades and told her son he was old enough to start taking care of himself. Russell was hospitalized once for attempting to hurt himself.

Bobby (age 13)

Bobby's parents died in a car accident when he was 10. With no relatives to take him in, Bobby was placed in a foster home. Because he had a severe speech impediment, possibly made worse by the trauma of losing his parents, he was ridiculed by his new family. People said he was retarded. Bobby began to act out and began an odyssey of more than twenty placements in foster and residential treatment homes. His speech impediment – one that was surgically correctable – was never diagnosed or treated.

Curtis (age 11)

Curtis looked a lot like his father who had walked out on his family several years before. Left on her own to care for four young children, his mother directed much of her bitterness and anger at Curtis. She often told him that his father was a "lazy bum" and that, since men were all alike, Curtis would be as worthless as his father. Curtis became disruptive and out of control. His mother told the other children not to talk or play with Curtis. She moved his bed and clothes into a small, unheated room in the basement. At age 10, he began running away for days at a time.

As you can see, every child who seeks help at Boys Town is a unique person with pain and suffering flooding his or her life. In many cases the pain and suffering is caused by others as in the case of physical, psychological, or sexual abuse. Yet there are other children whose parents did the very best they could to bring love and affection to their family but the child, for reasons unknown to anyone, began a life of involvement with drugs or truancy or shoplifting or many other antisocial behaviors. What makes Boys

Town such a special place is that we can help these children. We can give them hope. We do not always succeed – no one does – but we do believe you and I should never give up on a child.

Epilogue

*"There are no bad boys. There is only
bad environment, bad training,
bad example, bad thinking."*

—Father Edward Flanagan

Father Flanagan began to build Boys Town in
1917. The buildings have changed a lot over
the years as needs have changed, but the basic
message of hope remains the same. "There are
no bad boys." The boys and girls are not simply
to be blamed for their problems. They are to be
helped to overcome the bad influences in their
lives. They are all too often the products of "bad
environment, bad training, bad example, bad
thinking." They are to be helped by providing
them with better environment, better training,
better examples, and better thinking – better
reasons for being better and doing better.

Father Flanagan changed the way Americans
think about kids with problems. And, at Boys
Town, he provided an example of how his
message of hope could be put to work to help

youngsters. That example lives on today in the Family Homes on the Boys Town campus, in the Family Homes on the Boys Town USA mini-campuses, and in the Family Homes operated by organizations affiliated with Boys Town.

The better environment is the Family Home with live-in Family-Teachers and family-style surroundings of love and care. Better training is provided by the Family-Teachers who constantly teach the boys and girls new ways of dealing with the people and situations in their lives. The Family-Teachers and other staff are the better examples of how to behave in prosocial ways that elicit cooperation and warmth. And, better thinking can result from being in a helpful, supportive home with Family-Teachers who help the youngsters look at situations from several perspectives and generate many possible solutions to problems. "There are no bad boys." They are just kids who are growing up, and they need our help.

Helping the kids does not mean taking anything away from them. The young man who looks you in the eye, smiles, shakes your hand, and introduces himself at the door of a Family Home is quite capable of screaming, cursing, kicking, and hitting as violently as before he came to Boys Town. The young lady who calmly listens to her employer yell at her for being late to work, then quietly and rationally explains why as she apologizes, is still quite capable of becoming sullen and running away from a difficult situation as she had done many times before. They have not lost their old skills.

The secret is, they have acquired new skills. They now have two ways of dealing with life's situations: the old troublesome ways and the new healthy ways.

All of us are captives of our education. Kids in France grow up speaking French. Kids in Spain grow up speaking Spanish. Kids who grow up with "bad environment, bad training, bad examples, bad thinking" more often than not turn out to be "bad boys." They do what they have learned to do, what they have been taught to do, no matter how misguided or haphazard the teaching process may have been.

If kids are captives of their old education, they can also be captivated by a new education. French-speaking kids can learn German, and Spanish-speaking kids can learn Portuguese with the help of good teachers. "Bad boys" can learn more appropriate and socially acceptable ways of dealing with people and situations with the help of good Family-Teachers. They have not forgotten the old ways, but hopefully the old ways will fall into disuse as the kids learn new ways of living life. At least they will have a choice. And with the grace of God, they can choose life and goodness. If we can help them accomplish that, then the Boys Town Family Home Program will have done its job.

We thank you for listening to our story. We hope that you have a better understanding now of what makes Boys Town successful.

We also hope that you will spread the word about our unique system of child care. If there are residential facilities for youth in your area, why not share this book with them? Tell them that Boys Town has a program called the National Family Home Program which seeks to provide technical assistance to homes for children around the country, homes which wish to learn how to put Boys Town's quality care system in place in their own setting.

Index